Reading Peak 1

NE_Build & Grow

Unit Components

Student Book

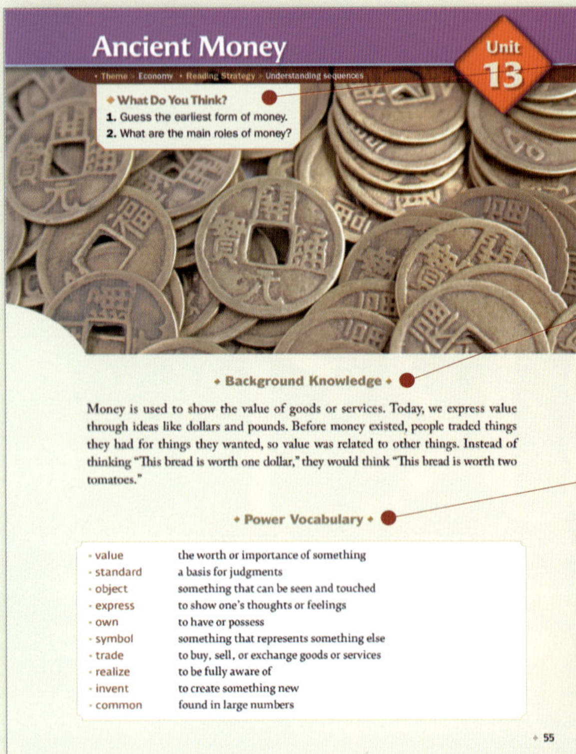
Ancient Money

Unit 13

• Theme • Economy • Reading Strategy • Understanding sequences

◆ What Do You Think?
1. Guess the earliest form of money.
2. What are the main roles of money?

◆ Background Knowledge ◆

Money is used to show the value of goods or services. Today, we express value through ideas like dollars and pounds. Before money existed, people traded things they had for things they wanted, so value was related to other things. Instead of thinking "This bread is worth one dollar," they would think "This bread is worth two tomatoes."

◆ Power Vocabulary ◆

· value	the worth or importance of something
· standard	a basis for judgments
· object	something that can be seen and touched
· express	to show one's thoughts or feelings
· own	to have or possess
· symbol	something that represents something else
· trade	to buy, sell, or exchange goods or services
· realize	to be fully aware of
· invent	to create something new
· common	found in large numbers

◆ 55

What Do You Think?

Simple warm up questions and related images stimulate students' interest in each topic.

Background Knowledge

Background information is presented to better prepare students for the main readings.

Power Vocabulary

Key words from the main reading passage are carefully chosen and defined to build up students' understanding of the context.

Reading Comprehension

Multiple-choice and short-answer questions are introduced to ensure the students' understanding of the passages.

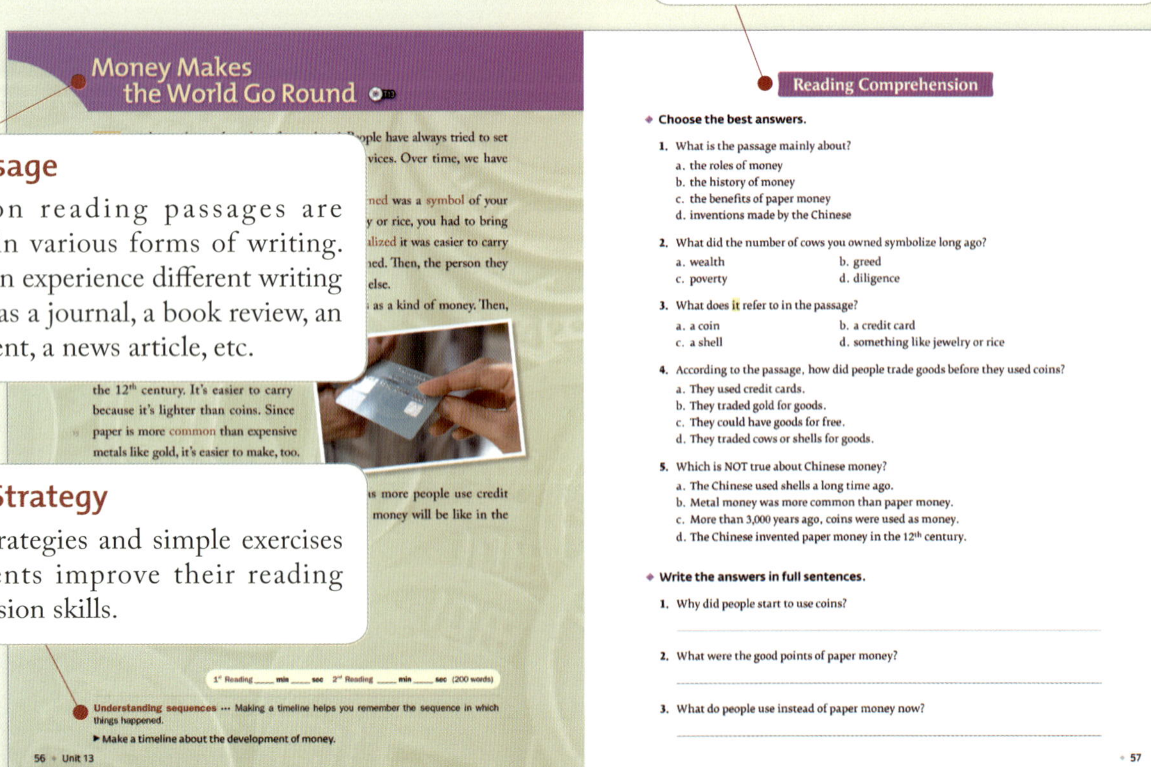
Money Makes the World Go Round

...ople have always tried to set ...vices. Over time, we have ...

...ned was a symbol of your ...y or rice, you had to bring ...alized it was easier to carry ...ned. Then, the person they ...else.

... as a kind of money. Then, ...

the 12th century. It's easier to carry because it's lighter than coins. Since paper is more common than expensive metals like gold, it's easier to make, too.

...s more people use credit ... money will be like in the ...

1st Reading ___ min ___ sec 2nd Reading ___ min ___ sec (200 words)

Understanding sequences ··· Making a timeline helps you remember the sequence in which things happened.

► Make a timeline about the development of money.

56 ◆ Unit 13

Reading Comprehension

◆ Choose the best answers.

1. What is the passage mainly about?
   a. the roles of money
   b. the history of money
   c. the benefits of paper money
   d. inventions made by the Chinese
2. What did the number of cows you owned symbolize long ago?
   a. wealth b. greed
   c. poverty d. diligence
3. What does it refer to in the passage?
   a. a coin b. a credit card
   c. a shell d. something like jewelry or rice
4. According to the passage, how did people trade goods before they used coins?
   a. They used credit cards.
   b. They traded gold for goods.
   c. They could have goods for free.
   d. They traded cows or shells for goods.
5. Which is NOT true about Chinese money?
   a. The Chinese used shells a long time ago.
   b. Metal money was more common than paper money.
   c. More than 3,000 years ago, coins were used as money.
   d. The Chinese invented paper money in the 12th century.

◆ Write the answers in full sentences.

1. Why did people start to use coins?
2. What were the good points of paper money?
3. What do people use instead of paper money now?

◆ 57

Main Passage

Nonfiction reading passages are presented in various forms of writing. Students can experience different writing styles such as a journal, a book review, an advertisement, a news article, etc.

Reading Strategy

Reading strategies and simple exercises help students improve their reading comprehension skills.

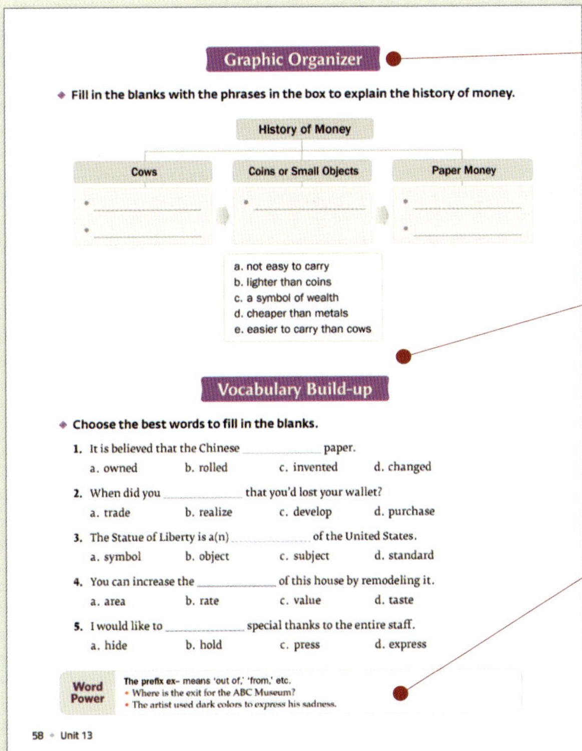

Graphic Organizer

◆ Fill in the blanks with the phrases in the box to explain the history of money.

History of Money

Cows	Coins or Small Objects	Paper Money
• ______	• ______	• ______
• ______	• ______	• ______

a. not easy to carry
b. lighter than coins
c. a symbol of wealth
d. cheaper than metals
e. easier to carry than cows

Vocabulary Build-up

◆ Choose the best words to fill in the blanks.

1. It is believed that the Chinese ______ paper.
   a. owned b. rolled c. invented d. changed
2. When did you ______ that you'd lost your wallet?
   a. trade b. realize c. develop d. purchase
3. The Statue of Liberty is a(n) ______ of the United States.
   a. symbol b. object c. subject d. standard
4. You can increase the ______ of this house by remodeling it.
   a. area b. rate c. value d. taste
5. I would like to ______ special thanks to the entire staff.
   a. hide b. hold c. press d. express

Word Power — The prefix ex- means 'out of,' 'from,' etc.
• Where is the exit for the ABC Museum?
• The artist used dark colors to express his sadness.

58 • Unit 13

Graphic Organizer

Graphic organizers help students summarize the information from the main reading passages logically.

Vocabulary Build-up

Additional multiple-choice questions further strengthen students' vocabulary acquisition.

Word Power

The uses of different prefixes, suffixes, and root words are explained with more examples.

Writing Practice

Grammar and writing practice enhance students' writing skills.

Workbook

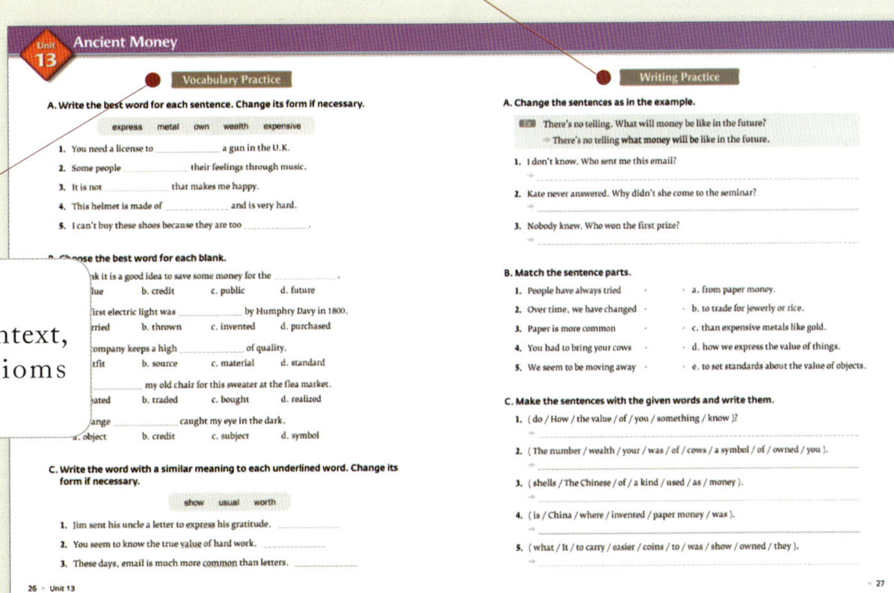

Vocabulary Practice

Exercises on new words in context, synonyms, antonyms, and idioms improve students' vocabulary.

Scope and Sequence

Mosquitoes

Unit 01

• Theme > Insects • Reading Strategy > Scanning

◆ **What Do You Think?**

1. When and where do you usually get bitten by mosquitoes?
2. What attracts mosquitoes?

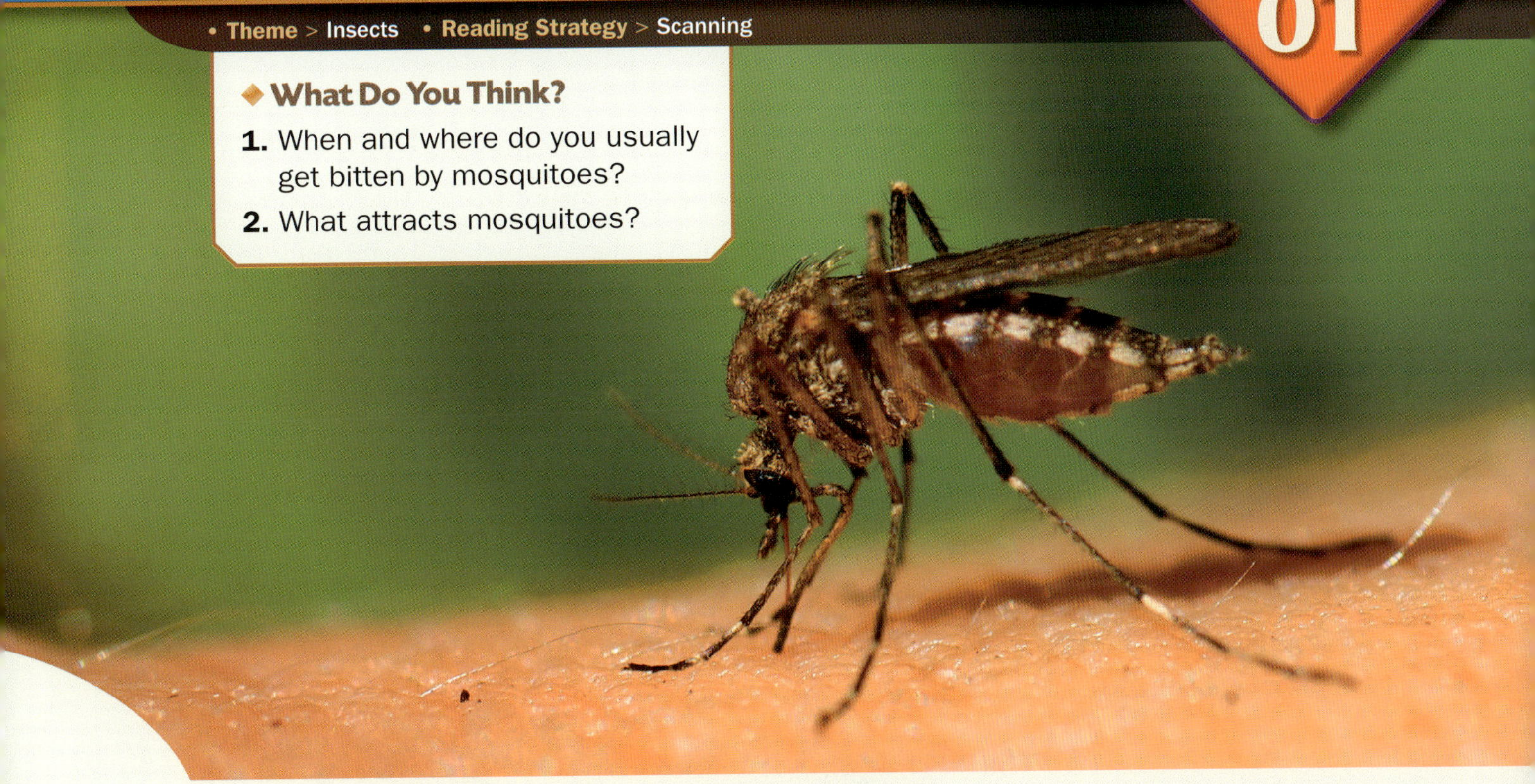

◆ Background Knowledge ◆

The word "mosquito" is Spanish for "little fly." This name was first used in North America in 1583. Even though the malaria mosquito is the best known type, there are about 3,500 different kinds of mosquitoes. There are small mosquitoes and big ones. Some are dangerous and fast, and some are harmless and lazy.

◆ Power Vocabulary ◆

• bite	to cut with the teeth
• spread	to send in all directions
• disease	a condition that causes harm to a living thing's health
• female	a woman or a girl
• produce	to make something
• attract	to draw by appealing to the emotions or senses
• sensor	anything that receives a signal and responds to it
• visual	relating to sight
• detect	to find or discover
• avoid	to keep away from

Flying Vampires

You have probably been bitten by a mosquito before. These bites can be dangerous. Mosquitoes spread diseases to more than 700 million people a year in Africa, South America, Central America, Mexico, and a large part of Asia. At least two million people die of these diseases each year. However, not all of them bite. It is only females that bite you. They bite because they need to drink blood to produce eggs. Here is some useful information about these flying vampires you might find helpful.

What attracts these female mosquitoes? They have three main sensors. First, using chemical sensors, mosquitoes can smell carbon dioxide up to 100 feet away. Certain chemicals in sweat also attract them.

Second, mosquitoes also have good visual sensors. If you move around while wearing bright colors, they can see you and will come straight for you!

Third, they have heat sensors, so they can detect heat. Since your body is warm, they can find you easily, even in the dark.

So what can you do? Avoid wearing clothes with bright colors in areas with many mosquitoes. And using mosquito nets and mosquito spray or lotion will keep mosquitoes far away from you. Having good luck will help, too!

1st Reading _____ min _____ sec 2nd Reading _____ min _____ sec (204 words)

Scanning ··· When you scan an article, you don't read every single word, just key words or ideas. This is helpful when searching for key information.

▶ What are the three main sensors of mosquitoes?

Reading Comprehension

◆ Choose the best answers.

1. What is the passage mainly about?
   a. ways to avoid mosquitoes
   b. different types of mosquitoes
   c. places where mosquitoes are found
   d. chemical sensors that mosquitoes have

2. What is true according to the passage?
   a. Female mosquitoes don't bite people.
   b. Mosquitoes carry diseases to a lot of people.
   c. When people are sweating, mosquitoes won't bite them.
   d. Clothes with bright colors protect people from mosquitoes.

3. Mosquitoes can smell ____________ from far away.
   a. blood　　b. carbon dioxide
   c. oxygen　　d. female mosquitoes

4. Which is NOT appropriate for the blank?

   Mosquitoes can detect people by using ____________ sensors.

   a. heat　　b. visual
   c. chemical　　d. hearing

5. Which is NOT a good way to avoid mosquitoes?
   a. exercising regularly　　b. using mosquito spray
   c. using mosquito nets　　d. avoiding wearing bright colors

◆ Write the answers in full sentences.

1. Why do female mosquitoes need to drink blood?

   ____

2. Which sensors help mosquitoes smell sweat?

   ____

3. What kinds of colors attract mosquitoes?

   ____

Graphic Organizer

◆ **Fill in the blanks with the phrases in the box to explain mosquitoes' sensors.**

Sensors of Mosquitoes

Chemical	Visual	Heat
• ______________	• ______________	• ______________

a. detect bright colors
b. find warm bodies easily
c. smell carbon dioxide and chemicals in sweat

Vocabulary Build-up

◆ **Choose the best words to fill in the blanks.**

1. The movie has excellent ______________ effects.
a. visual b. sweet c. bright d. chemical

2. I was standing under the roof to ______________ the rain.
a. hit b. bite c. avoid d. admit

3. The factory has tried to ______________ cheaper bottles.
a. drink b. attract c. produce d. experience

4. It is important to ______________ cancer in its early stages.
a. wear b. smell c. spread d. detect

5. The ______________ can be successfully treated if it is found early.
a. sweat b. blood c. sensor d. disease

Word Power

The root word –tract has the meaning of 'to pull,' 'to drag,' or 'to draw.'
- I could *extract* no information from him.
- Sean wants to break the *contract* between us.

Self-Care Technology

Unit 02

• Theme > Technology • Reading Strategy > Guessing word meaning

◆ **What Do You Think?**

1. How do you have your health checked?
2. What do you need to check your health?

Background Knowledge

Searching the Internet for information about health is a basic form of self-care, and it is very common. Now, companies are creating new kinds of technology, called self-care technology, which will help people monitor their health on their own. Some of these products seem unfamiliar, but they may become as normal as aspirin or vitamins someday.

Power Vocabulary

- snore — to breathe noisily during sleep
- rate — the number of times something happens over a period of time
- decide — to choose to do something
- exist — to be present
- record — to make note of
- information — facts about someone or something
- appointment — a meeting set in advance
- alert — to warn of possible danger
- notice — to pay attention
- aware — having knowledge or understanding

Health Helpers T02

When Emily woke up, she checked her phone and saw that she had snored the night before. Her phone also showed that she had moved a lot while she was sleeping. Another day, the monitor on her shirt showed that her heart rate was very fast. "It might be because I drink too much coffee," she thought. She decided not to have caffeine before bedtime any more.

It sounds like something from a science fiction book, but these "health helpers"—products for self-care—already exist. When you use them, they record information about you, such as your heart rate and body temperature. Then they can send this information to your doctor. If there's a problem, the doctor can make an appointment to see you in person. Or if there's an emergency, nurses or doctors will be alerted right away.

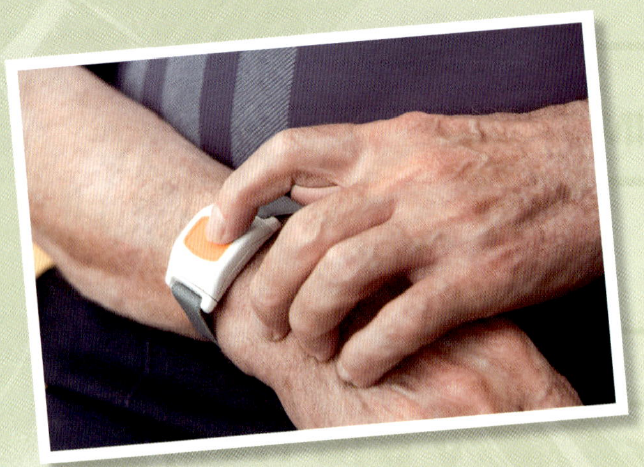

This is especially useful for people who have just had surgery or for elderly people who live alone. These products can also help prevent illness by teaching people about health issues. Serious illnesses often occur because people don't notice when they start to get sick. If people can easily check their own health, they might become more aware of their health. And then they can try to improve it on their own.

1st Reading ____ min ____ sec 2nd Reading ____ min ____ sec (213 words)

Guessing word meaning ··· When you see words you don't know, using a dictionary might take too much time and make it more difficult to understand the reading passage as a whole. Try to guess the meaning from the context.

▶ Guess the meaning of the word "emergency" in line **11**.

Reading Comprehension

◆ Choose the best answers.

1. What is the passage mainly about?

   a. ways to avoid caffeine
   b. the benefits of "health helpers"
   c. ways to cope with serious illness
   d. a convenient emergency alert system

2. "Health helpers" record people's ______________.

   a. daily diet
   b. surgery schedule
   c. heart rate
   d. doctor information

3. Which is NOT true about the "health helpers" described in the passage?

   a. They will be invented soon.
   b. People can easily check their health with them.
   c. They can show a body's condition while sleeping.
   d. They can send your health information to doctors.

4. "Health helpers" are especially useful for ______________.

   a. babies
   b. teenagers
   c. females
   d. elderly people

5. How can "help helpers" help people prevent illness?

   a. by performing surgery
   b. by taking care of elderly people
   c. by taking people to the hospital quickly
   d. by teaching people about health issues

◆ Write the answers in full sentences.

1. What kinds of information do "health helpers" show?

   ____

2. Who will get the health information checked by "health helpers"?

   ____

3. What happens when a person checked by "health helpers" has a problem?

   ____

Graphic Organizer

◆ **Choose the correct phrases from the box and fill in the blanks to explain the functions of "health helpers."**

Functions of "Health Helpers"

- ______________________________
- ______________________________
- ______________________________

a. perform surgery on patients
b. teach people about health issues
c. teach people ways to become a nurse
d. alert doctors in case of an emergency
e. record health information and send it to a doctor

Vocabulary Build-up

◆ **Choose the best words to fill in the blanks.**

1. I have an ______________ with my dentist at 3 p.m.

a. issue b. emergency c. information d. appointment

2. Drinking too much coffee will increase your heart ______________.

a. rate b. monitor c. disease d. temperature

3. The experts ______________ the public to the dangers of smoking.

a. decided b. snored c. alerted d. shouted

4. I'm ______________ of what you mean, but I can't agree with you.

a. full b. aware c. proud d. right

5. Most car accidents ______________ because of sleepiness.

a. take b. occur c. place d. avoid

Word Power

The suffix -ment is used to add the meaning of 'the state of being acted on.'

- The tax *payment* is due on January 31st.
- I have been studying the *movements* of the planets.

Earthworms

Unit 03

• **Theme** > Animals • **Reading Strategy** > Finding main ideas

◆ **What Do You Think?**

1. What do earthworms look like?

2. What do earthworms eat?

◆ Background Knowledge ◆

Earthworms live underground and are found all over the world. Their bodies are soft and can be brown, pink, or red. In the Philippines, there are blue earthworms, and the United Kingdom even has green ones! Earthworms have brains. They also have five hearts. They can be small— about 1 cm long. Or they can be very big— 4 m long!

◆ Power Vocabulary ◆

• soil	material on the earth in which plants can grow
• fertile	able to produce healthy plants
• absorb	to take in
• prepare	to make something ready
• flow	to move freely as if in a stream
• loose	not tight; not compact
• protect	to prevent something from being damaged
• recycle	to process things to be used again
• trash	anything useless
• nature	all the things in the world that are not made by people

Nature's Own Recycler

T03

Did you know that earthworms are good farmers? They work so hard to make rich soil that they can help plants grow better without using any chemical fertilizers.

Earthworms eat while they move through the earth. They don't eat food, but instead eat the soil. The soil moves through their bodies, and when it comes out again, it is very, very fertile! This soil can be easily absorbed and used by plants.

Earthworms are called "nature's plows," because they are good at breaking up hard soil by digging large burrows[1] in it. These burrows bring air far down into the soil. And they also allow rainwater to move organic nutrients down deep into the soil where the roots lie. Then the roots carry these nutrients to the plants' stems.

Earthworms prepare the soil for the rain, too. When it rains on "earthworm soil," the water goes into the ground. It doesn't flow away, because the soil is loose and full of burrows.

Earthworms also protect the environment by recycling trash! They eat trash, it moves through their body, and plant food[2] comes out.

Earthworms are truly more than farmers. They are nature's own recyclers!

1 burrow: a hole in the ground

2 plant food: any substance used to make soil more fertile

1st Reading _____ min _____ sec 2nd Reading _____ min _____ sec (194 words)

Finding main ideas ··· Each passage has one or more main ideas, which are the most important information in the reading. They are usually in the first paragraph.

▶ What is the main idea of this passage?

Reading Comprehension

Choose the best answers.

1. What is the passage mainly about?

a. the features of rich soil
b. the benefits of earthworms
c. the important roles of farmers
d. ways to protect the environment

2. Which is NOT true about earthworms?

a. They eat the soil.
b. They recycle trash.
c. They break up hard soil.
d. They absorb chemical fertilizers.

3. The ______________ bring air far down into the soil.

a. plants
b. tools
c. farmers
d. burrows

4. What does It refer to in the passage?

a. The root
b. The soil
c. The water
d. An earthworm

5. What can be the best conclusion from the passage?

a. Rich soil needs rain.
b. We have to make use of soil.
c. Earthworms are helpful to the environment.
d. Recycling trash is important for the environment.

Write the answers in full sentences.

1. Why are earthworms called "nature's plows"?

____

2. What allows rainwater to move down into the soil?

____

3. How do earthworms recycle trash?

____

Graphic Organizer

◆ **Fill in the blanks with the phrases in the box to explain the benefits of earthworms.**

Benefits of Earthworms

On Soil	On Plants	On Environment
• ______________	• ______________	• ______________

a. make plants nutritious by letting rainwater and air in
b. make the soil fertile by eating it and letting it back out
c. protect the environment by changing trash into plant food

Vocabulary Build-up

◆ **Choose the best words to fill in the blanks.**

1. Plants ______________ water and minerals through their roots.
a. dig b. break c. protect d. absorb

2. One of my upper teeth is ______________ and aching.
a. wet b. rich c. loose d. heavy

3. This dish doesn't take much time to ______________.
a. flow b. prepare c. release d. prohibit

4. This soil is ______________ enough to grow big healthy tomatoes.
a. full b. foggy c. fertile d. chemical

5. We need to ______________ paper for the environment.
a. make b. grow c. throw d. recycle

Word Power

The prefix pre– means 'before,' 'prior to,' 'in advance of,' 'in front of,' etc.
- I have no *previous* publishing experience.
- Wash your hands often to *prevent* infection.

Sleep Debt

Unit 04

• **Theme** > Health • **Reading Strategy** > Recognizing cause and effect

◆ What Do You Think?

1. How many hours do you usually sleep each night?
2. What would you be like if you didn't sleep for several days?

◆ Background Knowledge ◆

Sleep debt occurs when a person doesn't get enough sleep. There are two kinds of sleep debt. One is caused by partial sleep loss, and the other is caused by total sleep loss. Partial sleep loss happens when a person sleeps too little over a certain period of time. Total sleep loss happens when a person is kept awake for days or weeks.

◆ Power Vocabulary ◆

- **owe** — to have to pay or repay
- **allow** — to make it possible for someone to do something
- **lack** — something missing or needed
- **affect** — to have an influence on
- **irritable** — easily annoyed
- **fatigue** — loss of strength and energy from doing hard work
- **concentrate** — to give all one's attention to something
- **normal** — usual and common
- **debt** — something that one has to pay
- **recover** — to get well

Do You Owe Yourself Some Sleep?

T04

Magazine

Do you sleep enough? If you don't, you owe yourself some rest! A study was done on rats more than ten years ago. When rats weren't allowed to sleep, they died within three weeks.

Sleep is very important for humans, too. In fact, a lack of sleep can seriously affect the quality of our life. People who lose just one night's sleep are usually irritable and feel fatigue the next day. If they miss sleep for two nights, they can't concentrate. They also make mistakes while doing normal tasks. After three nights, they might see things that are not there, and won't know what is real anymore.

What about people who get only a few hours of sleep each night? This is still not good. The lost hours add up each day, just like debt! These people will need even more sleep to fully recover. And if sleep debt gets worse, things can get even more serious. Scientists say it can lead to relationship problems, high blood pressure, and even heart attacks.

Scientists don't fully understand what sleep is. Still, they're sure about some things. For example, sleep makes us restful and calm. It also helps the brain work better, so that we can think faster and more clearly.

1st Reading _____ **min** _____ **sec** **2nd Reading** _____ **min** _____ **sec** (209 words)

Recognizing cause and effect ··· The cause of an event is the reason something happens. The effect of an event is the result of what happened.

▶ What are the effects of sleep debt?

Reading Comprehension

Choose the best answers.

1. What is the passage mainly about?

a. how to sleep well
b. the effects of sleep debt
c. why rats need sleep
d. what makes people sleepy

2. Which is NOT true according to the passage?

a. Sleep debt can lead to heart attacks.
b. Rats that didn't sleep died within a few weeks.
c. Losing one night's sleep doesn't cause any problems.
d. Scientists don't fully understand what happens while we sleep.

3. Which is NOT mentioned as a result of serious sleep debt?

a. lung cancer
b. high blood pressure
c. heart attacks
d. relationship problems

4. Which is NOT appropriate for the blank?

Sleep makes people ______________.

a. think faster
b. feel fatigue
c. restful and calm
d. think more clearly

5. What can be the best conclusion from the passage?

a. People need to get enough sleep.
b. Scientists don't know about sleep.
c. Rats and humans have things in common.
d. Sleeping habits are different for each person.

Write the answers in full sentences.

1. What happens to a person who does NOT sleep for one night?

____

2. What happens if you do NOT sleep for more than three nights?

____

3. Why is it NOT good to sleep only a few hours each night?

____

Graphic Organizer

◆ **Fill in the blanks with the sentences in the box to summarize the passage.**

Sleep Debt

- **1st paragraph:** ______________________
- **2nd paragraph:** ______________________
- **3rd paragraph:** ______________________
- **4th paragraph:** ______________________

a. Rats missing sleep died in three weeks.
b. Sleeping only a few hours also cause serious problems.
c. No sleep for one or more nights affects the quality of life.
d. Science tells us that sleep influences our bodies and minds.

Vocabulary Build-up

◆ **Choose the best words to fill in the blanks.**

1. I'm tired from a(n) ____________ of sleep these days.
a. lack b. task c. science d. experience

2. Josh has become ____________ since his noisy neighbor moved in.
a. calm b. faster c. irritable d. restful

3. This area is only for staff members, so you are not ____________ to enter.
a. led b. added c. affected d. allowed

4. I can ____________ more on studying when I'm at the library.
a. move b. explain c. concentrate d. understand

5. If you take this medicine, you'll ____________ from the disease soon.
a. rest b. enjoy c. focus d. recover

Word Power

The prefix re– means 'again' and is used to indicate repetition.
- The water *cycle* is the continuous movement of water.
- You need to *recycle* waste, not just throw it away.

The Harlem Renaissance

Unit 05

• Theme > Culture • Reading Strategy > Guessing word meaning

◆ **What Do You Think?**

1. What do you know about Harlem?
2. What is the meaning of the word "renaissance"?

◆ Background Knowledge ◆

Langston Hughes, Booker T. Washington, Billie Holiday, and Lena Horne were all part of the Harlem Renaissance. This was a cultural movement in the 1920s and 1930s. It influenced African American literature, philosophy, art, music, and entertainment. Writers, artists, actors, and musicians all sent the same message to the world: We are not inferior.

◆ Power Vocabulary ◆

• movement	a series of activities in which many people work for a goal
• literature	stories, poems, and plays that are considered to have value as art
• proud	feeling happy about your achievements
• race	a group of people with the same skin color or physical features
• independent	not connected with or joined to anything else
• wit	ability to say or write thoughts in a clever and often funny way
• experiment	to try new ideas to find out what results they will have
• reflect	to show the existence or nature of something
• mood	the way that a group of people are feeling
• influence	a person or thing that has an effect on someone or something

A Social Revolution

T05

Harlem, a neighborhood in New York City, became the center of a growing black middle class at the beginning of the 20th century. It was here that the Harlem Renaissance, an important African American cultural movement, began. It was a period when African-Americans did many great things in the fields of art, music, and literature.

Zora Neale Hurston was a popular novelist during this period. She was proud of her race and believed black Americans could be free and independent. As she grew up, she wanted to tell the world about black culture. She became well known in the 1920s for her wit and folk writing style.

Langston Hughes was born in Missouri in 1902 and started writing poetry at the age of 13. As Langston entered university and began living in Harlem, he was inspired by jazz and blues music made by black people. This music helped him experiment with rhythm and free verse. He also tried to reflect the mood of the times in his work. Before long, he became an important part of the Harlem Renaissance, and spoke out in support of poor and homeless black people.

The Harlem Renaissance has ended, but its influence is still felt today in the arts, literature, society, and politics.

1st Reading _____ min _____ sec 2nd Reading _____ min _____ sec (209 words)

Guessing word meaning ··· You can guess the meaning of words from their context.

► What is the meaning of the word "inspired" in line **14**?

Reading Comprehension

Choose the best answers.

1. What is the passage mainly about?
   a. ways to become a novelist
   b. the bad effects of racism
   c. Harlem Renaissance writers
   d. the features of a black middle class

2. Which is NOT true about Zora Neale Hurston?
   a. She was proud of her race.
   b. She was born in Missouri in 1902.
   c. She believed black Americans could be free.
   d. She is well known for her wit and folk writing style.

3. What did Zora Neale Hurston want to explain in her works?
   a. white racism
   b. black culture
   c. western culture
   d. white middle class

4. ______________ helped Langston Hughes use rhythm and free verse.
   a. The arts
   b. Politics
   c. Pop music
   d. Jazz and blues music

5. Who did Langston Hughes speak out for?
   a. rich white people
   b. homeless white people
   c. poor white people
   d. homeless black people

Write the answers in full sentences.

1. When did Harlem become the center of a growing black middle class?

   ____

2. When did Zora Neale Hurston become well known?

   ____

3. What does the Harlem Renaissance still influence today?

   ____

Graphic Organizer

◆ **Fill in the blanks with the phrases in the box to explain the Harlem Renaissance.**

Writers of the Harlem Renaissance

Zora Neale Hurston	Langston Hughes
• ______________	• ______________
• ______________	• ______________
• ______________	• ______________

a. wanted to tell about black culture	b. experimented with rhythm and free verse
c. was inspired by jazz and blues music	d. became popular for her wit and writing style
e. started to write poetry at the age of 13	f. spoke out for poor and homeless black people

Vocabulary Build-up

◆ **Choose the best words to fill in the blanks.**

1. Parents ______________ their children's behavior.

a. appear b. prepare c. purchase d. influence

2. It is wrong to judge people by their ______________.

a. era b. pace c. race d. rate

3. Kelly's cheerful words put the classroom in a good ______________.

a. mood b. verse c. style d. motion

4. America became ______________ from Great Britain in 1783.

a. equal b. proud c. civil d. independent

5. The newspaper ______________ the opinions of the local people.

a. opens b. reflects c. becomes d. experiments

Word Power

The prefix in– is used to add an opposite meaning to some adjectives.
- The man made very *accurate* clocks.
- We don't need *inaccurate* information.

Ballet

Unit 06

• Theme > Performing arts • Reading Strategy > Understanding sequences

◆ **What Do You Think?**

1. Have you ever seen a ballet performance?
2. Do you know any ballet movements?

◆ Background Knowledge ◆

Did you know there are many different styles of ballet? The most formal style is classical ballet. It uses traditional ballet techniques to create graceful movements. To perform classical ballet, dancers must first learn five basic positions. They also need to develop strong legs and feet, so they can dance on their toes. Classical ballet is also different in different places. There is French ballet, Russian ballet, and Italian ballet.

◆ Power Vocabulary ◆

• evolve	to develop over time
• royalty	the power or position of a king or queen
• compete	to try to do better than another person or group
• impressive	capable of making a strong impact on the mind or emotions
• luxurious	special and expensive
• found	to start or build something, such as an institution, society, etc.
• instruct	to teach someone how to do something
• public	not private; open to the people as a whole
• establish	to create or set up
• nation	an organized body of people under a single government

The Dance of Royalty

T06

Ballet is one of the most popular forms of dance today. However, it has been around for a long time. It evolved from dances held for European royalty during the 16th century.

At that time, the royal families of France and Italy were competing to see who could have the most impressive shows. They would hold beautiful dance performances based on traditional folk dances. These were called *balletti*, the Italian word for "dance." Unlike folk dancing, these shows featured fancy costumes and backgrounds. The first ballet was held in 1581, at the luxurious wedding of the sister of the queen of France.

Later, the first school of dance was founded by King Louis XIV of France. It instructed dancers in the special skills needed for ballet. In 1669, the first opera house was opened in Paris. It featured ballet as part of the opera performances. This was the first time that ballet could be enjoyed by the public. The first ballet company was established at this opera house in 1713.

Today, ballet isn't just for European royalty. There are ballet companies in cities around the world. They perform this unique style of dance for people across classes and nations.

1st Reading _____ min _____ sec 2nd Reading _____ min _____ sec (199 words)

Understanding sequences ··· Stories are usually told in the order in which the events occurred — from beginning to ending.

► When was the first ballet company established?

Reading Comprehension

◆ Choose the best answers.

1. What is the passage mainly about?

a. the history of ballet
b. the skills of ballet dancers
c. French traditional culture
d. the opening of the first opera house

2. Which is NOT true according to the passage?

a. The first opera house was opened in Paris.
b. Ballet and opera were performed together in Paris.
c. Ballet was developed from traditional folk dancing.
d. The term ballet comes from the French word for "dance."

3. The first ballet was held when a French queen's sister got ______________.

a. hired
b. arrested
c. married
d. elected

4. What are the best words for (A) and (B)?

> King Louis XIV ______(A)______ a dance school to ______(B)______ ballet skills.

a. destroyed – share
b. visited – display
c. attended – explain
d. founded – teach

5. How could ballet be enjoyed by common people?

a. It was shown at an opera house.
b. It was taught at a public school.
c. It was performed by a king and a queen.
d. It was included in a traditional wedding.

◆ Write the answers in full sentences.

1. When was the first opera house started?

____

2. What did ballet evolve from in the 16th century?

____

3. How is ballet different from folk dancing?

____

Graphic Organizer

◆ **Fill in the blanks with the sentences in the box to explain ballet's development.**

Development of Ballet

1. ______________________________
2. ______________________________
3. ______________________________
4. ______________________________
5. ______________________________

a. The first ballet company was established.
b. King Louis XIV founded the first dance school.
c. Ballet was featured as a part of opera performances.
d. The first ballet was held at the wedding of a queen's sister.
e. The royal families of France and Italy hold dance performances called *balleti*.

Vocabulary Build-up

◆ **Choose the best words to fill in the blanks.**

1. The whole ______________ shouted with joy after winning a medal.

a. style b. nation c. tradition d. performance

2. The two runners are ______________ to see who is faster.

a. evolving b. deciding c. competing d. complaining

3. This hotel is expensive because the rooms are very ______________.

a. tiny b. public c. luxurious d. uncomfortable

4. I ______________ the new worker how to use the machine.

a. tried b. opened c. featured d. instructed

5. We decided to ______________ a recycling center in my hometown.

a. need b. establish c. learn d. drive

Word Power

The prefix com– is used to add the meaning of 'together,' 'with,' or 'fully.'
- Mike's cooking is good, but it can't *compare* with mine.
- We can't *communicate* with each other because of the different languages.

Life in Space

Unit 07

• Theme > Space • Reading Strategy > Distinguishing fact from opinion

◆ **What Do You Think?**

1. What are the differences between life in space and on the Earth?

2. Would you like to live in space?

◆ Background Knowledge ◆

Outer space is very different from the Earth. The differences can be good or bad! For example, in space you can't breathe without an oxygen mask because there is no air. What about jumping? In space, you can jump much further and much higher. Another good thing is that you can see the stars and planets better because there is no pollution in space!

◆ Power Vocabulary ◆

- astronaut — a person who is trained for traveling in a spacecraft
- effect — something that is produced by a cause
- gravity — the force which causes things to fall toward the center of the Earth
- float — to rest or move in a liquid or the air
- container — something that is used to hold or store things
- add — to join or unite something to something else
- atmosphere — the air in any given place
- control — to have a power over
- wipe — to rub for cleaning or drying
- tie — to fasten, connect or bind

Give Me Space! T07

The International Space Station (ISS) is like a big house in space. The astronauts don't feel the effects of gravity and float around the station. Their life in space is different from life on the Earth.

Astronauts eat the same food in space that people eat on the Earth. The food is in plastic containers, though. Sometimes they add water, and sometimes they heat it in an oven.

What about clothes? The atmosphere in the space station is controlled by computers, so astronauts dress the same way as people on the Earth. They wear special clothes only when traveling to and from the station on the space shuttle.

Astronauts need to wash themselves in space. Of course, there are no showers, baths, or faucets! So, they wipe their bodies clean with towels. Or they wash themselves with special soap that doesn't have to be rinsed off.

Sleeping is different in space, too. Astronauts sleep in sleeping bags in small rooms, but they have to tie themselves down before going to bed. Otherwise, they would float around the station!

It must be great living in space ... but only for a while. Imagine: no baths, no swimming pools, and no walks in the park!

1st Reading _____ min _____ sec 2nd Reading _____ min _____ sec (203 words)

Distinguishing fact from opinion ··· A fact is objective information. An opinion is a person's view, judgment, or attitude that cannot be proved.

► Underline the sentence which shows the writer's opinion.

Reading Comprehension

Choose the best answers.

1. What is the passage mainly about?

a. what life in space is like
b. how to make a space station
c. why people want to live in space
d. which foods are necessary for astronauts

2. Which is NOT mentioned about life in space?

a. food b. clothes c. laundry d. sleeping

3. Which is NOT true about the food astronauts eat in space?

a. They can only eat frozen food.
b. The food is stored in plastic containers.
c. Sometimes they heat the food in an oven.
d. They can enjoy the same food people eat on the Earth.

4. What do we need to do when we are in space?

a. We need to wash ourselves with water.
b. We always need to wear special clothes.
c. We need to learn the way to float around.
d. We need to tie ourselves down when we sleep.

5. How do astronauts wash themselves in space?

a. in baths b. with faucets
c. with towels d. with showers

Write the answers in full sentences.

1. Why do astronauts float around the space station?

____

2. When do the astronauts wear special clothes?

____

3. Where do astronauts sleep in the ISS?

____

Graphic Organizer

◆ **Fill in the blanks with the phrases in the box to explain life in space.**

Life in Space

Food	Clothes	Washing	Sleeping
• ________	• ________	• ________	• ________
________	________	________	________
• ________	• ________	• ________	• ________
________	________	________	________

a. use special soap	b. wipe body with towels
c. tie themselves down	d. add water or heat in an oven
e. sleep in sleeping bags	f. dress like people on the Earth
g. store in plastic containers	h. wear special clothes in certain cases

Vocabulary Build-up

◆ **Choose the best words to fill in the blanks.**

1. The ________ is already filled with water.
a. soap b. faucet c. clothes d. container

2. Apples fall from trees because of ________.
a. air b. effect c. water d. gravity

3. I ________ the window clean with a towel.
a. broke b. wiped c. heated d. rinsed

4. Ashley ________ the box with a red ribbon and gave it to me.
a. tied b. flied c. climbed d. floated

5. The ________ is becoming more polluted by smoke.
a. bath b. astronaut c. atmosphere d. astronomer

Word Power

The suffix –er is used to form nouns meaning a person or thing that performs an action.
- This drink doesn't *contain* any sugar.
- Store your food in this *container*.

Green City

Unit 08

• Theme > Social issues • Reading Strategy > Identifying an author's purpose

◆ **What Do You Think?**

1. Are there any environmental problems in your town?
2. What can you do to make your town greener?

◆ Background Knowledge ◆

A green city tries to protect the environment. It reduces pollution and energy use, recycles, and uses natural materials or recyclable materials. The results are usually good — the environment improves, the government saves a lot of money, and citizens learn about the importance of protecting the environment better. Stockholm, Vancouver, Copenhagen, and many other cities have joined this movement.

◆ Power Vocabulary ◆

• natural	existing in or made by nature
• pollution	the state of being harmful to living things
• balance	to create an equality in weight, parts, etc.
• environment	the natural world
• develop	to make something new
• area	a part of a town, a country, or the world
• function	what something is used for
• relationship	the way two things are connected
• improve	to make better
• solution	an answer to a problem or question

The Green Capital

T08

Magazine

Stockholm, Sweden is always green! That means it still has a great deal of natural beauty. Although Stockholm has used a lot of land to build buildings, most of the land is still free from pollution.

To balance the good of the environment and human well-being, the city of Stockholm has developed a "green map." This map has three

parts: areas for ecological protection, areas for recycling, and areas for human social functions. The city leaders planned the ecological protection areas very carefully. They tried to put these protected areas close to each other. As a result, animals can easily move from one area to another.

There is also a good relationship between green areas and the places where people live. For example, food waste from homes can be used to improve the soil in green areas. Also, the green areas make people's lives more comfortable, giving them a place for leisure and recreation.

One of the biggest lessons we can learn from the green map is that planning is important. Without planning, we couldn't have found good solutions for both the environment and humans. Using this kind of planning, more and more cities around the world can "go green"!

1st Reading _____ min _____ sec 2nd Reading _____ min _____ sec (200 words)

Identifying an author's purpose ··· Authors write texts for particular reasons. They may try to inform, educate, persuade, advertise or describe.

► What is the purpose of this article?

Reading Comprehension

Choose the best answers.

1. What is the passage mainly about?
   a. the importance of recycling
   b. planning a trip to Stockholm
   c. the bad effects of a green map
   d. creating an environmentally friendly city

2. Most of the land in Stockholm is free from ____________.
   a. humans
   b. plants
   c. recycling
   d. pollution

3. Which areas do NOT belong to Stockholm's "green map"?
   a. areas for recycling
   b. areas for human shelter
   c. areas for ecological protection
   d. areas for human social functions

4. Which is NOT mentioned about Stockholm?
   a. its population
   b. the usage of its food waste
   c. its natural beauty
   d. the elements of its green map

5. What is true about Stockholm's "green map"?
   a. It consists of four parts.
   b. Green areas can be used as amusement parks.
   c. Animals can't easily move from one wedge to another.
   d. It was developed to balance the environment and human well-being.

Write the answers in full sentences.

1. Why did Stockholm try to put the protected areas close to each other?

   ____

2. How does Stockholm use food waste from homes?

   ____

3. How do green areas help make people's lives more comfortable?

   ____

Graphic Organizer

◆ **Fill in the blanks with the sentences in the box to explain Stockholm's Green Map.**

Stockholm's Green Map		
Ecological Protection	**Recycling**	**Human Social Functions**
• ______________	• ______________	• ______________

a. Protected areas are put close each other.
b. People can have a place for leisure and recreation.
c. Food waste from homes is used to improve the soil.

Vocabulary Build-up

◆ **Choose the best words to fill in the blanks.**

1. A wise person can ______________ work and play.
a. develop b. balance c. produce d. confuse

2. I've had a close ______________ with Angela since the age of 13.
a. energy b. protection c. well-being d. relationship

3. The city is trying to find ______________ for its problems.
a. results b. questions c. solutions d. pollution

4. This refrigerator has a fast cooling ______________.
a. land b. leader c. function d. recycling

5. This ______________ has had serious floods for the last decade.
a. area b. map c. plan d. lesson

Word Power

The suffix **-ship** is used to add the meaning of 'condition,' 'character,' or 'skill.'
• There is no *relation* between the two events.
• Our *relationship* is getting worse every day.

Xylitol

Unit 09

• Theme > Health • Reading Strategy > Recalling facts and details

◆ **What Do You Think?**

1. Have you seen any products containing xylitol?
2. Is xylitol gum helpful to your health?

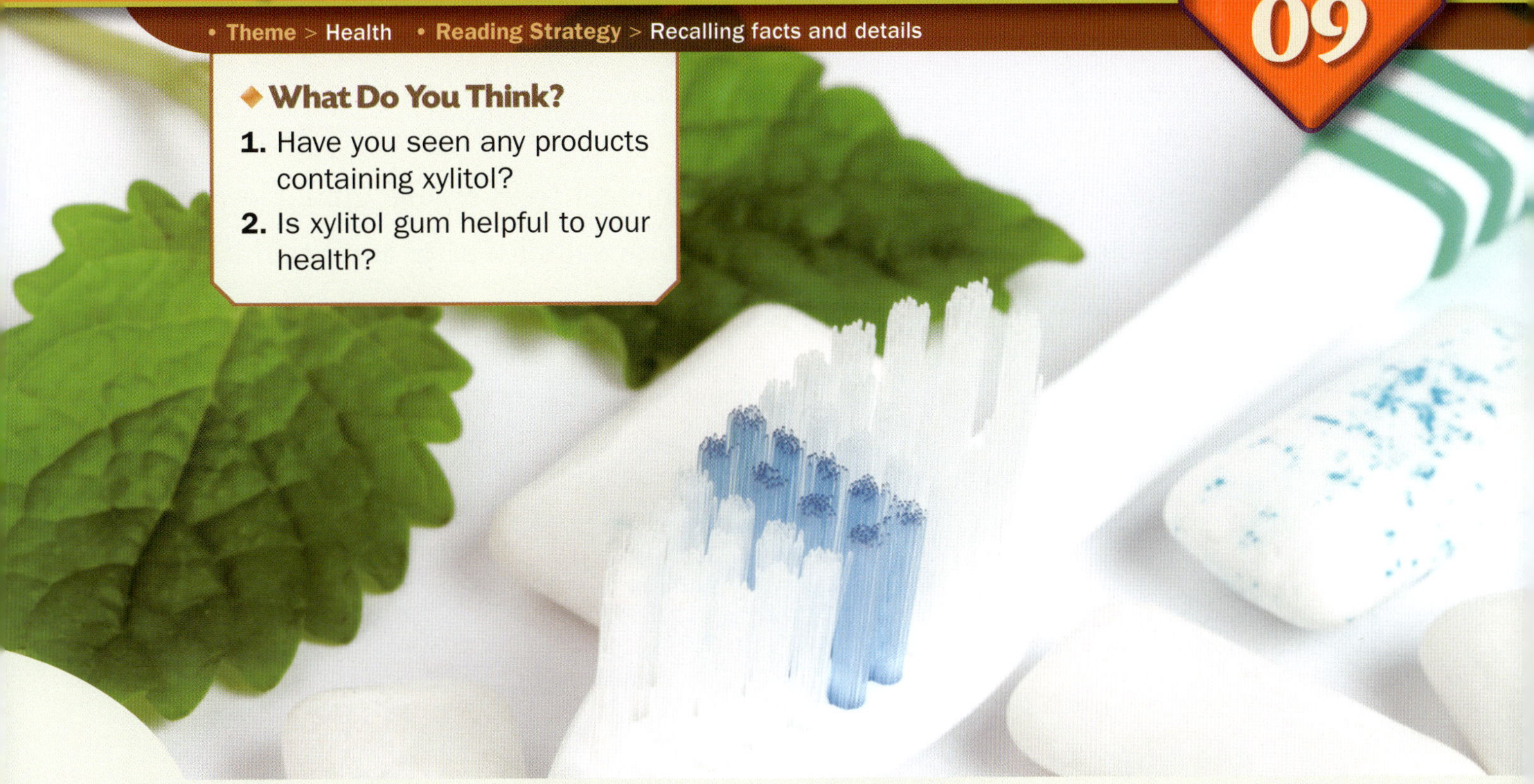

◆ Background Knowledge ◆

Sugar is usually not seen as a healthy ingredient in food. Luckily, there is a better version. Xylitol is a healthy substitute for regular white sugar. It is found naturally in some foods, such as corn, plums, and mushrooms. It tastes exactly like regular white sugar but contains only two thirds of the calories.

◆ Power Vocabulary ◆

- chew — to crush with the teeth
- regular — normal or usual
- discover — to find out
- benefit — something that is good
- research — work of studying something and discovering facts about it
- prevent — to keep from happening
- decay — the process of breaking down or becoming destroyed
- infection — a disease caused by germs or bacteria
- material — the substance of which a thing is made
- prove — to make clear that something is true

Chewing Toward Health

T09

Have you ever chewed gum made with xylitol? How did it taste? You probably didn't think it tasted any different from regular gum. However, there is one major difference. Gum made with xylitol is safer and healthier for the human body than gum made with sugar. This is why many gum companies use xylitol.

Xylitol was first discovered in the late 19th century by German and French chemists. It has a sweet taste but fewer calories than regular white sugar. Also, it doesn't affect blood sugar levels. So xylitol is popular among people with diabetes[1].

By the mid-20th century, scientists found other benefits of xylitol. In research, it was shown to prevent tooth decay and help fight infections. The materials in xylitol fight off harmful bacteria and make the teeth healthier. Toothpaste, chocolate, gum, and other products with xylitol in them keep us healthy. For example, regularly washing one's nose with a spray containing xylitol decreases the number of bacteria in it, preventing infections.

Since its discovery, sugar lovers have liked xylitol for its taste. And it has been proven to be safe and healthy. So next time you chew gum, how about trying some made with xylitol?

1 diabetes: a disease in which the sugar level in a person's blood is too high

1st Reading _____ min _____ sec 2nd Reading _____ min _____ sec (199 words)

Recalling facts and details ··· Facts and details include more examples and more explanation of the main statement. These can explain meaning of a word or give statistics.

► Underline the examples of the uses of xylitol.

Reading Comprehension

Choose the best answers.

1. What is the passage mainly about?

a. ways to treat diabetes
b. the ingredients in xylitol
c. the health benefits of xylitol
d. the harmful effects of xylitol

2. Xylitol was discovered ______________ by German and French chemists.

a. before the 19th century | b. in the late 19th century
c. in the mid-20th century | d. in the late 20th century

3. Why is xylitol popular among people with diabetes?

a. because it contains white sugar
b. because it doesn't taste like gum
c. because it helps you lose weight
d. because it doesn't affect blood sugar levels

4. Which is NOT true about xylitol?

a. It causes tooth decay.
b. It helps fight infections.
c. Its materials make teeth healthier.
d. It can be used in toothpaste and gum.

5. What product can prevent nose infections?

a. xylitol sprays | b. xylitol chocolate
c. xylitol candies | d. xylitol toothpaste

Write the answers in full sentences.

1. Why do many gum companies use xylitol?

____

2. Why is xylitol healthier than regular white sugar?

____

3. What benefits of xylitol had been found by the mid-20th century?

____

Graphic Organizer

◆ Choose the correct phrases from the box and fill in the blanks to explain health benefits of xylitol.

Health Benefits of Xylitol

- ______________________________
- ______________________________
- ______________________________

a. helps fight infections
b. affects blood sugar levels
c. increases the number of bacteria
d. prevents diabetes and tooth decay
e. has fewer calories than regular sugar

Vocabulary Build-up

◆ Choose the best words to fill in the blanks.

1. Toothpaste helps prevent tooth ____________.

a. ache b. decay c. tastes d. benefits

2. My teacher helped me ____________ my talents.

a. forget b. affect c. prevent d. discover

3. Keep in mind you can't ____________ gum during the class.

a. add b. chew c. create d. swallow

4. Karl had to stay alone to prevent ____________ from others.

a. disorder b. research c. diabetes d. infection

5. The latest study ____________ that everyone was wrong.

a. calls b. proves c. appears d. influences

Word Power

The prefix dis– has the meaning of 'apart,' 'away,' or a negative force.

- I *dislike* carrots and mayonnaise.
- I am really good at *distinguishing* different smells.

Musical Instruments

Unit 10

• Theme > Music • Reading Strategy > Classifying information

◆ **What Do You Think?**

1. What kinds of instruments do you like best?
2. What is the most important thing in an orchestra, and why?

◆ Background Knowledge ◆

Orchestras were first developed in Europe hundreds of years ago. Now they can be seen and heard all over the world. Little has changed since their beginning. The standard of orchestras is still defined by the involvement of string, wind, and percussion instruments. How many instruments are included from each group depends on the size of an orchestra.

◆ Power Vocabulary ◆

• wonder	to think about with curiosity
• instrument	an object used to produce music
• modern	of the present or recent time
• harmony	the pleasant combination of notes sounded at the same time
• string	thin rope
• confuse	to mistake one thing for another
• blow	to send out air from the mouth
• vibrate	to shake or move from side to side
• variety	a number or collection of different things
• attend	to be present at

The Harmony of an Orchestra

T10

Have you ever listened to an orchestra and wondered what kinds of musical instruments were being played? There are three groups of instruments in a modern orchestra. String, wind, and percussion instruments are played in harmony to create beautiful music.

The violin, viola, cello, and bass are string instruments. They are made of wood and each has four strings. All four-stringed instruments are played the same way: by plucking[1] or drawing a bow across the strings.

There are two types of wind instruments: brass and woodwinds. People may confuse the two. The sound of woodwinds, like the oboe and the flute, is created when the player blows into at least one reed[2]. The players cover holes with their fingers to make sounds. The sound of brass instruments, such as the trumpet, comes from the player's lips vibrating against the mouthpiece.

The third group in an orchestra is the percussion instruments. They produce a sound when hit, shaken or rubbed. Some examples of percussion instruments are cymbals, the timpani, and the xylophone.

These three groups of instruments come together wonderfully with their variety of sounds to make an orchestra. The next time you attend an orchestra concert, don't forget to take a close look at the instruments.

1 pluck: to play by pulling out

2 reed: a small piece of cane or metal inserted into the mouthpiece of a woodwind instrument

1st Reading ____ min ____ sec 2nd Reading ____ min ____ sec (206 words)

Classifying information ··· Classifying is to put things into groups according to their characteristics.

► How are instruments grouped in a modern orchestra?

Reading Comprehension

Choose the best answers.

1. What is the passage mainly about?
   a. the long history of orchestras
   b. different types of string instruments
   c. ways to play in harmony in an orchestra
   d. the main instruments of modern orchestras

2. Which is NOT appropriate for the blank?

   The instruments of modern orchestras can be divided into three groups: ______________, ______________, and ______________ instruments.

   a. string　　b. wind　　c. electric　　d. percussion

3. Which is NOT an example of a string instrument?
   a. violin　　b. cello　　c. viola　　d. trumpet

4. What is true according to the passage?
   a. There are three types of wind instruments.
   b. Oboes and flutes are examples of woodwinds.
   c. String instruments are played by blowing into a reed.
   d. Wind instruments are played by drawing a bow across strings.

5. Percussion instruments produce a sound when hit, shaken or ______________.
   a. blown　　b. rubbed　　c. plucked　　d. vibrated

Write the answers in full sentences.

1. How are string instruments played?

   ____

2. How is the sound of brass instruments created?

   ____

3. What are examples of percussion instruments?

   ____

Graphic Organizer

◆ **Fill in the blanks with the phrases in the box to classify the instruments.**

Three Groups of Instruments

	Strings	Winds	Percussion
Instruments	• ____________	• ____________	• ____________
How to Play	• ____________	• ____________	• ____________

a. oboe, flutes, trumpets
b. hit, shake or rub
c. cymbals, timpani, xylophones
d. violin, viola, cello, bass
e. blow into a reed or cover holes
f. pluck or draw a bow across the strings

Vocabulary Build-up

◆ **Choose the best words to fill in the blanks.**

1. People often ____________ me with my twin sister.
a. tell b. confuse c. wonder d. vibrate

2. The Scottish army used to play ____________ called bagpipes.
a. sounds b. materials c. performances d. instruments

3. Our team won the first prize because of our perfect ____________.
a. meals b. fight c. holes d. harmony

4. Please let me know if you cannot ____________ the meeting.
a. blow b. listen c. attend d. forget

5. Anne majors in classical dance but she likes ____________ dance, too.
a. future b. modern c. outdated d. old-fashioned

Word Power

The prefix con– has the meaning of 'with' or 'together.'
- Don't *confuse* the two instruments.
- It is too early to *conclude* that John is the thief.

Yellow Dust

Unit 11

• Theme > Nature • Reading Strategy > Recognizing cause and effect

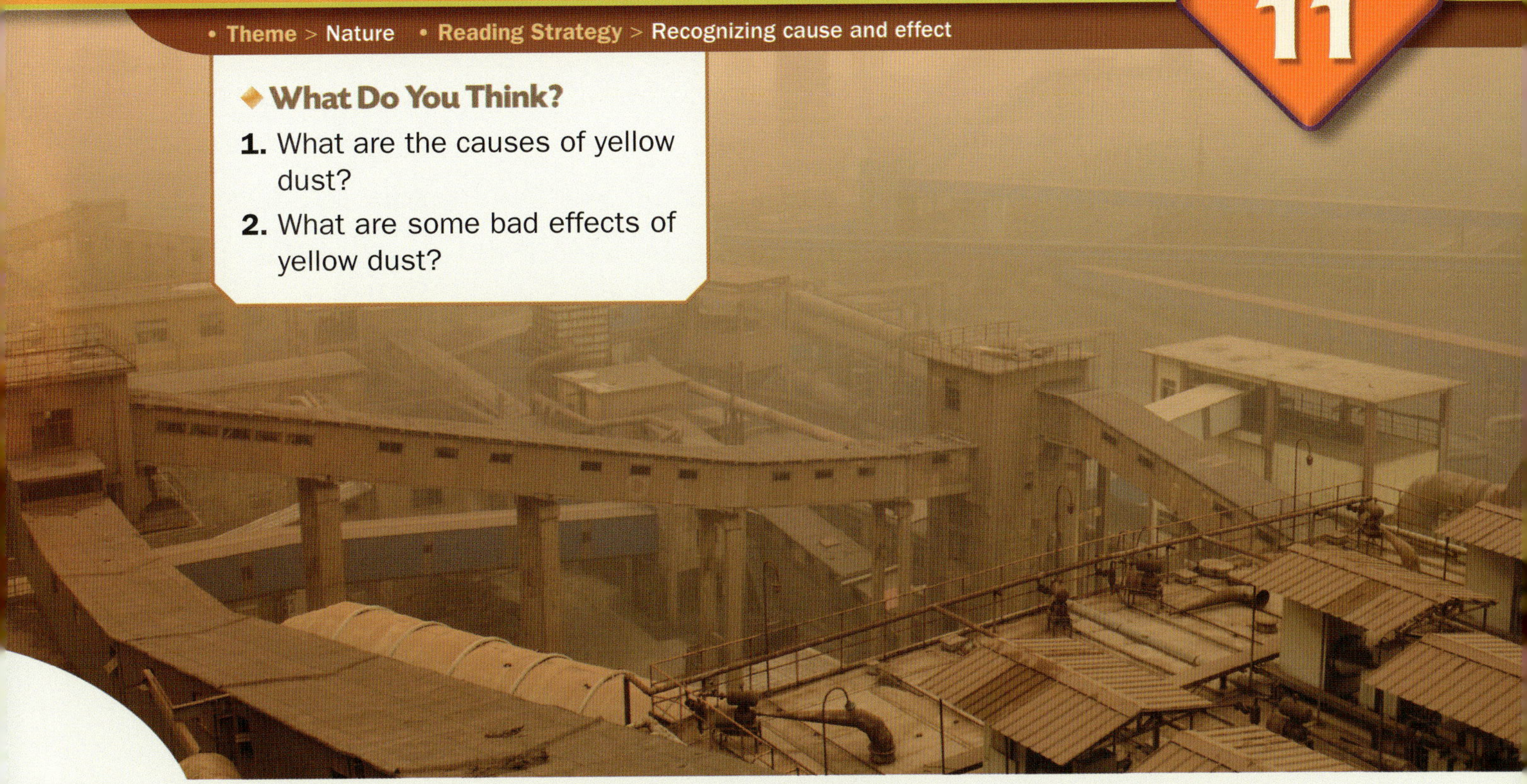

◆ What Do You Think?

1. What are the causes of yellow dust?
2. What are some bad effects of yellow dust?

◆ Background Knowledge ◆

Yellow dust is the name of a storm that occurs in Asian countries every year in the spring. The first record of yellow dust in Korea comes from 174 AD, during the Silla Dynasty. The dust was called "raining sands." People thought it was sent from the sky by an angry god. Today, we use the names "yellow dust," "Asian dust," or "China dust storms."

◆ Power Vocabulary ◆

- carry — to take from one place to another
- harmful — having a bad effect
- ash — the grey powder that remains after something has burned
- poisonous — capable of killing or causing sickeness
- occur — to take place or happen
- illness — an unhealthy condition
- destroy — to cause much damage
- habitat — the natural environment where an animal or plant lives
- cost — to require the payment of money
- major — great in number, size, or amount

Blanketed in Yellow Dust

T11

Yellow dust comes from the Gobi Desert in southern Mongolia and northern China, usually in the spring. The wind carries the dust over China, Korea, and Japan. It is unwelcome because of its many harmful effects on people's health, the environment, and even the economy.

Yellow dust is full of pollution such as ash and poisonous gases and metals. It also carries viruses and bacteria. When the dust goes into the nose and the lungs, many problems can occur, such as a sore throat or breathing difficulties. People even die of illnesses that are caused by yellow dust.

The dust can also harm the environment by ruining the soil and creating acid rain. It destroys animals' habitats, too.

Yellow dust storms cost people a lot of money, as well. It can take up to 6,000 gallons of water to clean one jumbo jet after a major dust storm.

So, how can we deal with yellow dust? Some people wear masks when they go outside. Others stay home from work or school to avoid breathing the bad air. In order to control the dusty weather, China started to plant more trees, hoping to change the deserts into forest lands. However, planting trees is not enough. We also need to cut down on pollution.

1st Reading _____ min _____ sec 2nd Reading _____ min _____ sec (212 words)

Recognizing cause and effect ··· To determine the cause, ask the question "Why did it happen?" To determine the effect, ask the question "What happened?"

▶ Underline the effects of yellow dust.

Reading Comprehension

Choose the best answers.

1. What is the passage mainly about?

   a. famous desert areas
   b. ways to clean jumbo jets
   c. bad effects of yellow dust
   d. illnesses caused by yellow dust

2. Which is NOT affected by yellow dust?

   a. industry　　b. the economy
   c. people's health　　d. the environment

3. Which is NOT true about yellow dust?

   a. It cures a sore throat.
   b. It contains poisonous metals.
   c. It carries viruses and bacteria.
   d. Some people die of illnesses caused by it.

4. Which is NOT appropriate for the blank?

   Yellow dust affects the environment by ____________.

   a. ruining the soil　　b. cleaning polluted air
   c. creating acid rain　　d. destroying animals' habitats

5. What is mentioned as a way to deal with yellow dust?

   a. staying outside　　b. wearing sunglasses
   c. planting more trees　　d. opening windows for fresh air

Write the answers in full sentences.

1. Where does yellow dust come from?

   ____

2. What is yellow dust full of?

   ____

3. How much water is needed to clean one jumbo jet after a dust storm?

   ____

Graphic Organizer

◆ Fill in the blanks with the phrases in the box to explain the harmful effects of yellow dust.

Harmful Effects of Yellow Dust

On People's Health	On the Environment	On the Economy
• ____________ • ____________	• ____________ • ____________ • ____________	• ____________

a. ruins the soil	b. destroys animals' habitats
c. creates acid rain	d. causes breathing difficulties
e. causes a sore throat	f. costs a lot to clean after a dust storm

Vocabulary Build-up

◆ Choose the best words to fill in the blanks.

1. Alcoholism can ____________ people's lives.
   a. avoid b. pollute c. destroy d. control
2. It is not easy to find wildlife in its natural ____________.
   a. economy b. habitat c. history d. pollution
3. The ____________ reason I quit my job was my health problem.
   a. sore b. major c. enough d. expensive
4. ____________ materials must be kept away from children.
   a. Sore b. Cold c. Sick d. Poisonous
5. Regular exercise can help you recover from your ____________.
   a. toxic b. grade c. illness d. health

Word Power

The prefix inter– is used to add the meaning of 'between' or 'within.'
- I'm taking an *intermediate*-level class.
- Don't *interrupt* me until I finish this drawing.

Fruits and Vegetables

Unit 12

• Theme > Food • Reading Strategy > Recalling facts and details

◆ What Do You Think?

1. What are your favorite fruits and vegetables?
2. What are the health benefits of eating fruits and vegetables?

◆ Background Knowledge ◆

People need fruit and vegetables in their daily diet. They are the best source of vitamins, minerals, fiber, and natural medicine. Experts say that most people don't eat enough of them, though. They say we need 1-2 cups of fruit and 3-4 cups of vegetables each day. We can eat them fresh, frozen, canned, dried or juiced — but fresh is the best!

◆ Power Vocabulary ◆

• plain	simple; without patterns especially in color
• contain	to have within
• nutrient	substance that helps plants and animals grow
• role	what something is used for
• reduce	to cut down on
• risk	possibility of loss or misfortune
• strengthen	to make something healthier and stronger
• ability	power to do something
• include	to put in as part of a set, group, or category
• pregnant	having a baby growing in one's body

A Rainbow of Health

T12

Do you like your food colorful or plain? Food scientists say you must eat different colored fruits and vegetables every day. The different colors contain different nutrients, and they play different roles.

Red fruits and vegetables contain lycopene, which reduces the risk of cancer. It also protects your body cells and your heart. Foods in this group are red apples, red peppers, cranberries, pink grapefruit, tomatoes, and watermelon.

Orange and yellow fruits and vegetables fight against cancer, and they help make your eyes healthy. They also strengthen your body's ability to help prevent sickness. Yellow apples, peaches, oranges, papayas, yellow peppers, and pumpkins are a few healthy examples.

Green fruits and vegetables include plant chemicals that help you avoid eye diseases. They are also good for pregnant mothers. Try some fruits such as green apples, avocados, green grapes, and kiwi fruit. Or try some vegetables such as green beans, broccoli, lettuce, green peppers, and spinach.

Do you like plums, blueberries, purple grapes, and eggplants? These blue and purple fruits and vegetables protect the body cells and help prevent heart disease. They improve memory, too!

White fruits and vegetables like bananas, garlic, onions, potatoes, and mushrooms improve cholesterol levels and blood pressure. They also fight against stomach cancer and heart disease.

1st Reading _____ min _____ sec 2nd Reading _____ min _____ sec (210 words)

Recalling facts and details ··· Nonfiction passages include facts and details which support the main idea. They include examples and explanations on the main statement.

▶ Underline the examples in each paragraph.

Reading Comprehension

Choose the best answers.

1. What is the passage mainly about?

a. nutrients that people need
b. various ways to prevent diseases
c. ways to choose healthy vegetables
d. roles of different fruits and vegetables

2. Which is NOT mentioned about red fruits and vegetables?

a. They harm body cells.
b. They contain lycopene.
c. They help avoid cancer.
d. Red peppers and cranberries are in this group.

3. Which is NOT true about orange and yellow fruits and vegetables?

a. They improve memory.
b. They help eyes stay healthy.
c. They help fight against cancer.
d. They include papayas and pumpkins.

4. ______________ fruits and vegetables are good for pregnant mothers.

a. Red b. Orange c. Green d. Purple

5. Which is appropriate for the blank?

______________ help improve cholesterol levels and blood pressure.

a. Onions b. Mangos c. Plums d. Carrots

Write the answers in full sentences.

1. What do green fruits and vegetables include that helps people avoid eye disease?

____

2. What fruits and vegetables help people remember things better?

____

3. What are examples of blue and purple fruits and vegetables?

____

Graphic Organizer

◆ **Fill in the blanks with the phrases in the box to explain benefits of different colored fruits and vegetables.**

Benefits of Different Colored Fruits and Vegetables

Red	Orange & Yellow	Green	Blue & Purple	White
• ______ ______	• ______ ______	• ______ ______	• ______ ______	• ______ ______

a. improve memory
b. make eyes healthy
c. reduce the risk of cancer
d. improve cholesterol levels
e. are good for pregnant mothers

Vocabulary Build-up

◆ **Choose the best words to fill in the blanks.**

1. Both coffee and tea ______ caffeine.
a. eat b. play c. contain d. improve

2. A research study showed that yogurt ______ bones.
a. lifts b. avoids c. includes d. strengthens

3. Kathy plays an important ______ in the movie.
a. role b. risk c. scene d. ability

4. The company ______ the number of workers to cut costs.
a. hired b. reduced c. produced d. increased

5. When planning your diet, try to choose foods with lots of ______.
a. cells b. illness c. diseases d. nutrients

Word Power

The suffix -en changes adjectives or nouns into verbs.
• Judy doesn't have the *strength* to run.
• I try to *strengthen* my relationship with my partner.

Ancient Money

Unit 13

• **Theme** > Economy • **Reading Strategy** > Understanding sequences

What Do You Think?

1. Guess the earliest form of money.
2. What are the main roles of money?

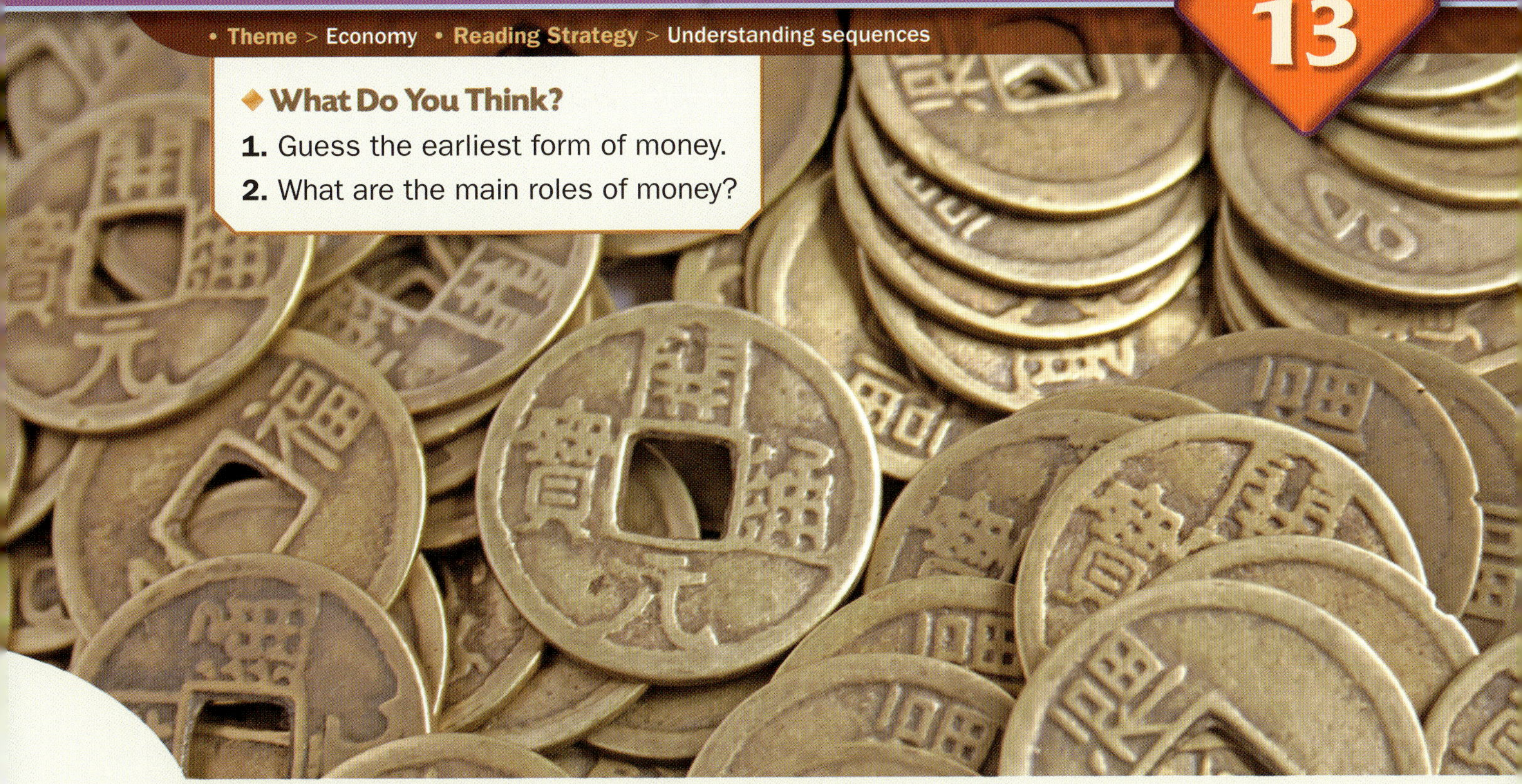

Background Knowledge

Money is used to show the value of goods or services. Today, we express value through ideas like dollars and pounds. Before money existed, people traded things they had for things they wanted, so value was related to other things. Instead of thinking "This bread is worth one dollar," they would think "This bread is worth two tomatoes."

Power Vocabulary

• value	the worth or importance of something
• standard	a basis for judgments
• object	something that can be seen and touched
• express	to show one's thoughts or feelings
• own	to have or possess
• symbol	something that represents something else
• trade	to buy, sell, or exchange goods or services
• realize	to be fully aware of
• invent	to create something new
• common	found in large numbers

Money Makes the World Go Round

T13

How do you know the value of something? People have always tried to set standards about the value of objects and services. Over time, we have changed how we express the value of things.

A long time ago, the number of cows you owned was a symbol of your wealth. If you wanted to buy something like jewelry or rice, you had to bring your cows to trade for it. As time went by, people realized it was easier to carry coins or other small objects to show what they owned. Then, the person they gave these coins to could use them to get something else.

Long ago, for instance, the Chinese used shells as a kind of money. Then, more than 3,000 years ago, they started to use coins. China is also where paper money was invented, in the 12th century. It's easier to carry because it's lighter than coins. Since paper is more common than expensive metals like gold, it's easier to make, too.

Money is still changing. Now we seem to be moving away from paper money, as more people use credit cards and Internet banking. There's no telling what money will be like in the future.

1st Reading ____ min ____ sec 2nd Reading ____ min ____ sec (200 words)

Understanding sequences ··· Making a timeline helps you remember the sequence in which things happened.

▶ Make a timeline about the development of money.

Reading Comprehension

◆ Choose the best answers.

1. What is the passage mainly about?

a. the roles of money
b. the history of money
c. the benefits of paper money
d. inventions made by the Chinese

2. What did the number of cows you owned symbolize long ago?

a. wealth
b. greed
c. poverty
d. diligence

3. What does it refer to in the passage?

a. a coin
b. a credit card
c. a shell
d. something like jewelry or rice

4. According to the passage, how did people trade goods before they used coins?

a. They used credit cards.
b. They traded gold for goods.
c. They could have goods for free.
d. They traded cows or shells for goods.

5. Which is NOT true about Chinese money?

a. The Chinese used shells a long time ago.
b. Metal money was more common than paper money.
c. More than 3,000 years ago, coins were used as money.
d. The Chinese invented paper money in the 12th century.

◆ Write the answers in full sentences.

1. Why did people start to use coins?

____

2. What were the good points of paper money?

____

3. What do people use instead of paper money now?

____

Graphic Organizer

◆ **Fill in the blanks with the phrases in the box to explain the history of money.**

History of Money

Cows	Coins or Small Objects	Paper Money
• ______________ • ______________	• ______________	• ______________ • ______________

a. not easy to carry
b. lighter than coins
c. a symbol of wealth
d. cheaper than metals
e. easier to carry than cows

Vocabulary Build-up

◆ **Choose the best words to fill in the blanks.**

1. It is believed that the Chinese ______________ paper.
a. owned   b. rolled   c. invented   d. changed

2. When did you ______________ that you'd lost your wallet?
a. trade   b. realize   c. develop   d. purchase

3. The Statue of Liberty is a(n) ______________ of the United States.
a. symbol   b. object   c. subject   d. standard

4. You can increase the ______________ of this house by remodeling it.
a. area   b. rate   c. value   d. taste

5. I would like to ______________ special thanks to the entire staff.
a. hide   b. hold   c. press   d. express

Word Power

The prefix ex– means 'out of,' 'from,' etc.
• Where is the exit for the ABC Museum?
• The artist used dark colors to *express* his sadness.

Social Network Service

Unit 14

• Theme > Social issues • Reading Strategy > Comparing and contrasting

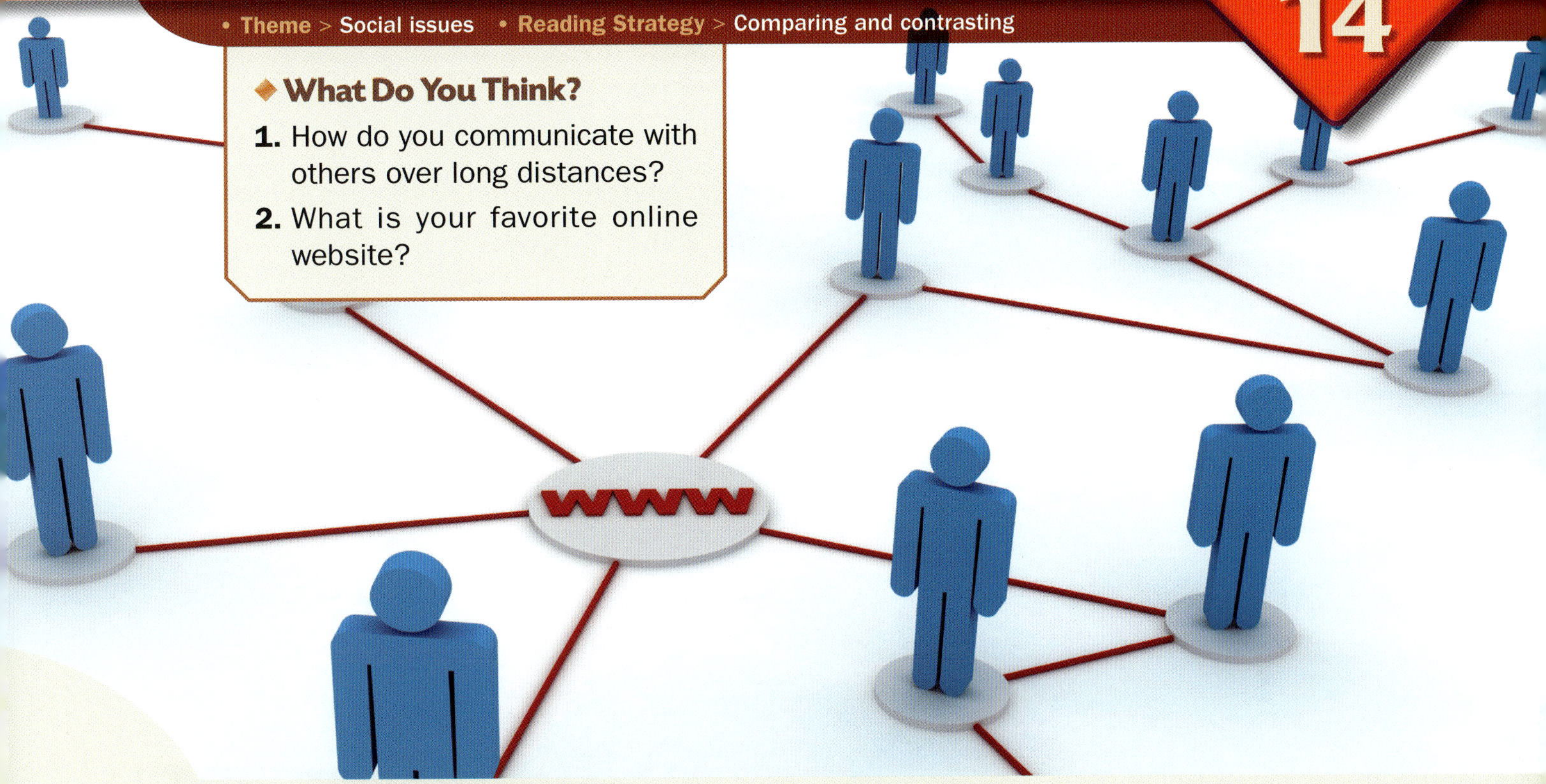

◆ What Do You Think?

1. How do you communicate with others over long distances?
2. What is your favorite online website?

◆ Background Knowledge ◆

A social network service (SNS) is a kind of website which allows its users to share their thoughts, ideas, photographs, and videos with one another online. The users can create their own social networks with people who have the same interests and hobbies as they do. These services, such as Facebook and Twitter, are now extremely popular all around the world.

◆ Power Vocabulary ◆

• social	meeting people and forming relationship with them
• support	to give help to
• effort	something done by hard work
• chat	to talk in a light manner
• share	to have in common; communicate
• broadcast	to make widely known
• personal	belonging or relating to a particular person and no one else
• post	to place images or information in a public place
• view	to look at or watch something
• border	a line separating two things

Building Worldwide Connections

T14

You might not know the term "social network service (SNS)." But you probably use one every day! The idea started in the 1990s. People began to form Internet communities to support their efforts to meet new people. Users would communicate by chatting and sharing photos online.

Eventually, these sites developed into SNSs. Today, they are easier to use and have better features. Currently, it is thought that there are over 200 active SNSs. Two of the most popular ones are Facebook and Twitter. These services allow people to broadcast their thoughts in "real time." This means that as soon as they think of something, they can share it with everyone who is part of their social network.

Not only is this kind of technology a lot of fun, but also it helps people build stronger personal relationships. However, there are some problems. Users must be careful about what kind of information they post to SNSs. It may seem like you're chatting only with a close friend. But in fact, your message can be viewed by thousands of people you might not know.

In spite of privacy issues, SNSs have become an important part of many people's lives. By creating an online world without borders, they make it easy for us to connect and share information with anyone, anywhere, anytime.

1st Reading ____ min ____ sec 2nd Reading ____ min ____ sec (220 words)

Comparing and contrasting ··· Comparing and contrasting is used to show how things or ideas are similar or different from one another.

▶ How are Internet sites today different from the ones in the 1990s?

Reading Comprehension

Choose the best answers.

1. What is the passage mainly about?

a. the origin of the Internet
b. a new way to communicate
c. ways to share photos online
d. the dangers of online shopping

2. What has developed into SNSs?

a. Twitter　　b. broadcasting system
c. Facebook　　d. Internet communities

3. What are the best words for (A) and (B)?

> Messages posted on SNSs may seem like ____(A)____ conversations, but they can be ____(B)____.

a. legal – illegal　　b. personal – public
c. free – expensive　　d. convenient – difficult

4. SNSs make it easy for people to ________ with anyone, anywhere, anytime.

a. work　　b. study　　c. connect　　d. compete

5. Which is NOT true according to the passage?

a. SNSs solved their privacy issues.
b. Facebook and Twitter are kind of SNSs.
c. Users of SNSs should be careful about what they post.
d. People began forming Internet communities in the 1990s.

Write the answers in full sentences.

1. Why did people begin to form Internet communities?

____

2. What does it mean to share a thought in "real time"?

____

3. What are the two most popular SNSs today?

____

Graphic Organizer

◆ **Fill in the blanks with the sentences in the box to explain features and problem of SNSs.**

SNSs	
Features	**Problem**
• ______________________	• ______________________
• ______________________	
• ______________________	

a. Privacy is not likely to be protected.
b. SNSs create an online world without borders.
c. People can build stronger personal relationships through SNSs.
d. People can broadcast their thoughts in "real time" through SNSs.

Vocabulary Build-up

◆ **Choose the best words to fill in the blanks.**

1. My salary is too low to ______________ my big family.
a. post b. allow c. share d. support

2. I want to discuss something ______________ with you.
a. slow b. quick c. careful d. personal

3. I lay on the ground and ______________ the stars.
a. meant b. viewed c. appeared d. connected

4. I spent the evening ______________ with my friend from Germany.
a. chatting b. explaining c. competing d. complaining

5. We're just two kilometers from the ______________ between China and Russia.
a. part b. edge c. border d. reality

Word Power

The suffix -al is used to add the meaning of 'having the character of' to nouns.
• Our school is proud of its 150 years of *tradition*.
• This handmade carpet is produced by *traditional* methods.

Art Therapy

Unit 15

• **Theme** > Psychology • **Reading Strategy** > Drawing conclusions

◆ What Do You Think?

1. What is the purpose of art?
2. How could art help people with mental or physical problems?

◆ Background Knowledge ◆

During World War II, there were many people who were troubled by the violence and stress around them. Most of these patients were going through a special kind of pain that was difficult to treat with common medical treatments. At this time, some doctors discovered that art could be used as therapy to help these patients.

◆ Power Vocabulary ◆

• mentally	in or with the mind
• physically	with the body
• cure	to restore to health or good condition
• heal	to make healthy
• deal	to handle or solve a problem
• figure	to come to understand by thinking carefully
• repeat	to do, make or perform again
• gradually	little by little
• ease	to make comfortable or give rest to
• receive	to get something given to you

Painting a Brighter Future

T15

Since the beginning of human civilization, art has had a strong influence on society. It is hard to find anything unrelated to art in our lives today. We often enjoy various forms of it in our leisure time. Amazingly, art can also be used to treat mentally and physically sick people.

In the mid-20th century, people thought that art could be used to help patients. And it is still being developed and studied as a way to cure patients today. Therapists use paintings to heal patients' various sicknesses. Painting with creative tools like paint brushes, and drawing with chalk and markers help patients deal with stress. The paintings show how they feel and what their physical or mental health is like. Using this art work, the therapists try to figure out their problems. Sometimes patients who have a hard time expressing themselves with words can freely express themselves in their paintings. Repeating this process gradually eases their problems as well.

Through art therapy, people have less stress and pain, and express themselves more freely. It is thought to be one of the best forms of therapy because it doesn't have any harmful side effects. Also, it is a fun activity that can help pass the time while patients receive medical treatment.

1st Reading _____ min _____ sec 2nd Reading _____ min _____ sec (211 words)

Drawing conclusions ··· When you draw conclusions, you often need to combine your knowledge with the information the author gives you.

▶ What conclusion did you draw from the passage?

Reading Comprehension

Choose the best answers.

1. What is the passage mainly about?

a. various uses of art
b. the roles of art therapy
c. ways to deal with stress
d. ways to become an art therapist

2. Which is NOT mentioned about art?

a. Art can be found all around us.
b. Art is not helpful for physical problems.
c. Art can be used to treat mental problems.
d. We enjoy various forms of art in our leisure time.

3. Art therapists use ______________ to cure patients.

a. movies
b. books
c. exercise
d. paintings

4. What is appropriate for the blank?

Art therapy helps patients ______________.

a. lose their memory
b. hide their feelings
c. show artistic talent
d. deal with their stress

5. What do the paintings created by patients NOT show?

a. their feelings
b. what their physical health is like
c. their medical records
d. what their mental health is like

Write the answers in full sentences.

1. When did people start to use art to help patients?

____

2. How can painting help patients deal with stress?

____

3. Why is art therapy thought to be one of the best forms of therapy?

____

Graphic Organizer

◆ **Fill in the blanks with the phrases in the box to show how art therapy works.**

How Art Therapy Works

Patients	Art Therapists
• ______________________	• ______________________
• ______________________	• ______________________

a. paint or draw with various tools
b. deal with problems without harmful effects
c. figure out patients' problems through their art work
d. show their feelings and what their physical or mental health is like

Vocabulary Build-up

◆ **Choose the best words to fill in the blanks.**

1. I didn't ______________ the package that I ordered last week yet.

a. cure　　b. paint　　c. receive　　d. express

2. Jamie ______________ the same mistake over and over again.

a. eased　　b. repeated　　c. stopped　　d. planned

3. Stella is physically healthy, but ______________ she is not healthy.

a. bodily　　b. mentally　　c. medically　　d. possibly

4. The doctor says it will take a long time to ______________ my neck problem.

a. heal　　b. drew　　c. care　　d. prove

5. Nick exercises regularly and he is ______________ losing weight.

a. rarely　　b. clearly　　c. suddenly　　d. gradually

Word Power

The suffix –ly forms adverbs from adjectives.
- Tim studied about *mental* illness.
- You have to be *mentally* healthy.

Threatened Oceans

Unit 16

• **Theme** > Environment • **Reading Strategy** > Recognizing cause and effect

◆ What Do You Think?

1. What causes the oceans to be polluted?
2. What problems does ocean pollution cause?

◆ Background Knowledge ◆

The ocean covers more than 71% of the Earth. It is considered the most important geographic feature in the world. Since it makes up more than half of the planet, it affects rainfall, the climate, and winds. Plants and animals living in the water are also influenced by the ocean. So even a little damage to our oceans can create a large problem for our world.

◆ Power Vocabulary ◆

• increase	to make greater in size, degree, number, etc.
• threaten	to be likely to harm
• spill	material that accidentally flows out of a container
• release	to let something fall; to set free
• extreme	of the greatest possible degree
• climate	the weather conditions of an area
• drought	a shortage of rainfall
• damage	any harm that reduces value or usefulness
• situation	a condition of things
• dump	to get rid of someone or something

S.O.S. – Save Our Seas

T16

Editorial

In the Mediterranean Sea, there are an increasing number of jellyfish. These jellyfish eat the food of other animals and have destroyed the balance of the ecosystem. So why are there so many jellyfish? It's because fishermen have caught too many Atlantic bluefin tuna, which eat jellyfish.

Humans have also threatened the Earth's oceans and seas in other ways. When the Suez Canal was built, for example, it introduced many non-native species to the waters of the Mediterranean Sea. Native species find it difficult to survive when they have to compete with non-native species.

Additionally, there have been a large number of oil spills in oceans and seas around the world. Also, factories release harmful materials into the sea. Many sea animals have died because of these spills and waste.

Extreme changes in climate, such as floods or droughts, have also created serious problems for a variety of ocean creatures.

Although the negative effects of human activities and climate change cannot be easily fixed, we can prevent further damage from happening. People need to understand the dangerous situations our oceans face. If we take just one step, such as no longer dumping waste into the sea, we might be able to save our oceans.

1st Reading ____ min ____ sec 2nd Reading ____ min ____ sec (204 words)

Recognizing cause and effect ··· The cause is what makes the effect happen. To identify cause and effect, look for clue words.

▶ What are the causes of sea pollution?

Reading Comprehension

◆ **Choose the best answers.**

1. What is the passage mainly about?
   a. effects of oil spills
   b. causes of sea pollution
   c. effects of human activities
   d. ways to protect native species

2. What caused an increase in the number of jellyfish?
   a. deaths of sea animals
   b. overfishing of bluefin tuna
   c. overfishing of jellyfish
   d. decreasing food for jellyfish

3. Which is NOT a cause threatening the oceans?
   a. waste from factories
   b. oil spills in the ocean
   c. the decrease of sea animals
   d. the introduction of non-native species

4. Extreme climate change, like floods or ______________, creates serious problems for ocean creatures.
   a. spills
   b. balance
   c. droughts
   d. factories

5. What is mentioned as a way to save the oceans?
   a. preventing climate change
   b. stopping all human activities
   c. not dumping waste into the sea
   d. understanding the importance of native species

◆ **Write the answers in full sentences.**

1. How do non-native species affect the ocean?

   ____

2. How does an increasing number of jellyfish affect the ecosystem of the ocean?

   ____

3. How can people prevent further damage to our oceans?

   ____

Graphic Organizer

◆ **Fill in the blanks with the sentences in the box to summarize the passage.**

Threats to Oceans

- **1st paragraph:** ______________________________
- **2nd paragraph:** ______________________________
- **3rd paragraph:** ______________________________
- **4th paragraph:** ______________________________
- **5th paragraph:** ______________________________

a. People have to take action to save our oceans.
b. Extreme climate changes create problems for ocean creatures.
c. Many sea animals die because of oil spills and harmful materials.
d. Introducing non-native species makes it hard for native species to survive.
e. The overfishing of certain fish has destroyed the balance of the ecosystem.

Vocabulary Build-up

◆ **Choose the best words to fill in the blanks.**

1. The storm caused great ______________ to the crops.
a. damage b. flood c. droughts d. promises

2. Most people ______________ half a liter of gas a day.
a. fix b. relate c. prevent d. release

3. The man ______________ people with sticks and stones.
a. lead b. dealt c. spilled d. threatened

4. The ______________ heat had a bad effect on farming.
a. bitter b. extreme c. negative d. natural

5. The company decided to cut the price to ______________ sales.
a. show b. decrease c. increase d. introduce

Word Power

The prefix in– is used in verbs, meaning 'into,' 'in,' 'on,' 'upon,' etc.
- My boss promised to *increase* my salary.
- The whole country came under the *influence* of the typhoon.

Check Your Reading Speed

Draw a bar on the table below indicating the speed of your 1st and 2nd reading of the main passages.

Reading Peak Book 1

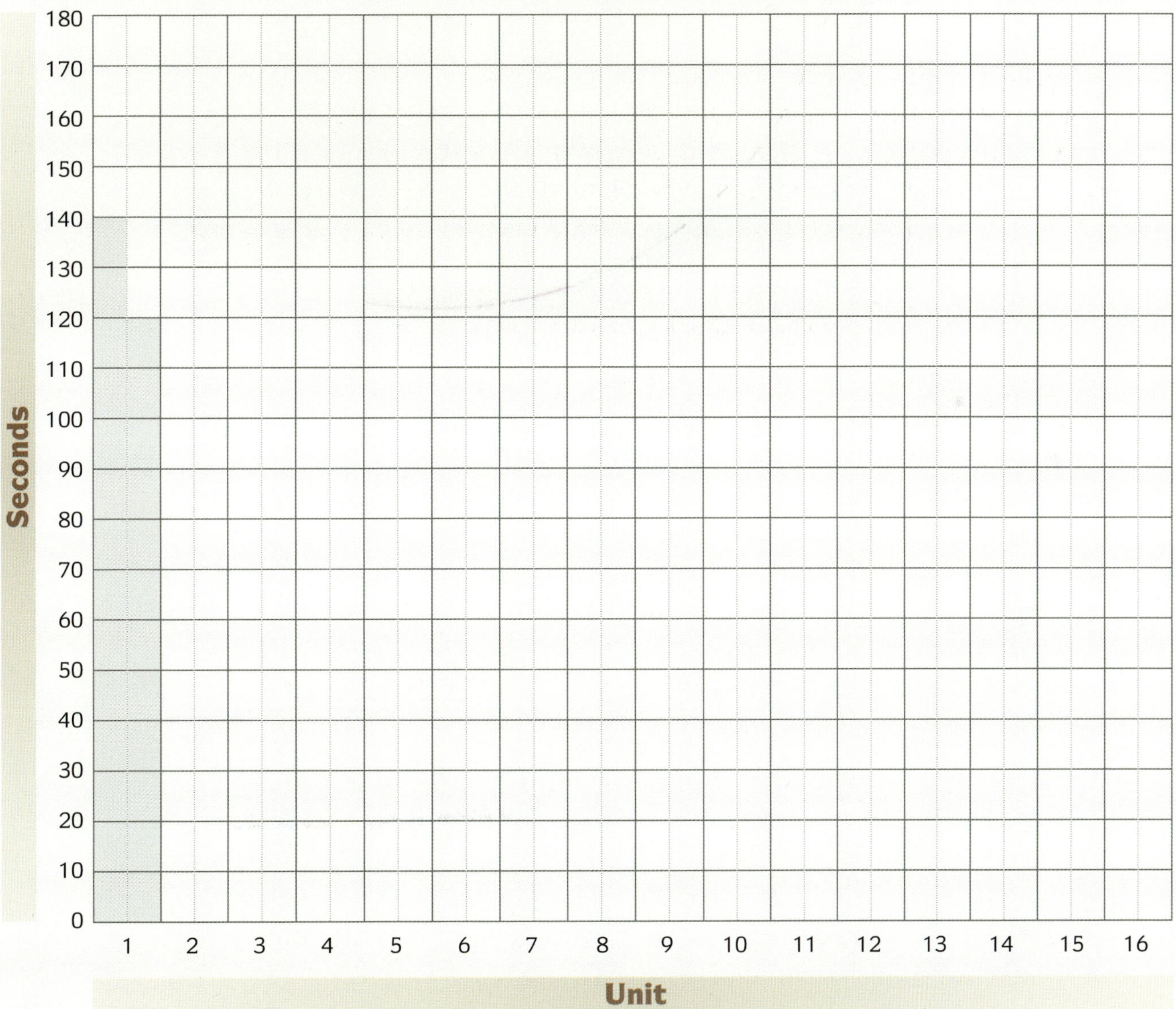

LEVEL GUIDE NE_Build & Grow Products

Category	Level: Books	Level: Lexile®	Kindergarten	Primary: Low Beginner	Primary: Beginner	Primary: High Beginner	Primary: Low Intermediate	Primary: Intermediate	Primary: High Intermediate	Secondary: A	Secondary: B	Components
Phonics	Phonics Show 1,2,3,4											Student Book/ Workbook/ 2 MultiROMs
	Phonics Show Readers 1,2,3,4											Book/ Audio CD
	Come On, Phonics 1, 2, 3, 4, 5											Student Book/ Workbook/ Readers/ DVD-ROM
Readers	Show Time L1,2,3											Student Book/ Workbook/ MultiROM
Coursebook	Come On, Everyone 1,2,3,4,5,6											Student Book/ Workbook/ Teacher's Book / DVD-ROM
Reading	Reading Sketch Starter 1,2,3	BR										Student Book/ Workbook/ MultiROM
	Reading Sketch 1,2,3	170L~210L										Student Book/ Workbook/ Audio CD
	Reading Sketch Up 1,2,3	260L~300L										Student Book/ Workbook/ Audio CD
	Reading Sponge 1,2,3	160L~280L										Student Book/ Workbook/ MultiROM
	Read & Retell 1,2,3	240L~390L										Student Book/ Workbook/ Audio CD
	Reading Sense 1,2,3	320L~410L										Student Book/ Workbook/ Audio CD
	Reading Clue 1,2,3	490L~510L										Student Book/ Workbook/ Audio CD
	The Basic Way 1,2,3 (2nd Edition)	570L~660L										Student Book/ Workbook/ MultiROM
	Read to Reach 1,2,3	600L~660L										Student Book/ Workbook/ Audio CD
	The Best Way 1,2,3 (2nd Edition)	860L~970L										Student Book/ Workbook/ MultiROM
	Reading Source 1,2,3	580L~710L										Student Book/ Workbook/ Audio CD
	Reading Peak 1,2,3	860L~900L										Student Book/ Workbook/ Audio CD
	Read Up 1,2,3	1070L~1320L										Student Book/ Supplementary Material/ MP3 CD
	Easy Link Starter 1,2,3											Student Book/ Workbook/ MultiROM
	Easy Link 1,2,3	240L~280L										Student Book/ Workbook/ MultiROM
	Easy Link 4,5,6	320L~380L										Student Book/ Workbook/

WORKBOOK

Reading Peak 1

NE_Build & Grow

WORKBOOK

Reading Peak 1

NE_Build & Grow

Unit 01

Mosquitoes

Vocabulary Practice

A. Write the best word for each sentence. Change its form if necessary.

bite sensors attract chemicals female

1. Be careful! That dog might ______________ you.
2. These ______________ can fight against cancer.
3. The band has male and ______________ singers.
4. There are ______________ on the door to prevent theft.
5. The restaurant prepard a new menu to ______________ more customers.

B. Choose the best word for each blank.

1. Please look ______________ ahead when you drive.
   a. low b. high c. tight d. straight
2. It is so hot outside that I can't take the ______________.
   a. color b. heat c. snow d. darkness
3. After running for one hour, my shirt was wet with ______________.
   a. tear b. spray c. sweat d. lotion
4. The rumor ______________ rapidly all over the town.
   a. speed b. treat c. spread d. throw
5. In spite of his hardships, Colin tries to look on the ______________ side.
   a. dark b. warm c. bright d. wrong

C. Write the word with a similar meaning to each underlined word. Change its form if necessary.

find section escape

1. You cannot smoke in the non-smoking area. ______________
2. This software will detect viruses on your computer. ______________
3. The criminal hid in the forest to avoid the police. ______________

Writing Practice

A. Change the sentences as in the example.

Ex *Only females* bite you.

→ **It is** only females **that** bite you.

1. My father bought me *a new watch*.

→ ____________________

2. I take *swimming class* on Saturdays.

→ ____________________

3. Susie ate a *sandwich and a salad* for lunch.

→ ____________________

B. Match the sentence parts.

1. Mosquitoes spread diseases •
2. At least two million people die •
3. Using chemical sensors, •
4. Avoid wearing clothes •
5. Mosquitoes have heat sensors, •

• a. so they can detect heat.
• b. with bright colors.
• c. of these diseases each year.
• d. mosquitoes can smell carbon dioxide.
• e. to more than 700 million people a year.

C. Make the sentences with the given words and write them.

1. (find / in / even / Mosquitoes / you, / the dark / can).

→ ____________________

2. (sweat / also / mosquitoes / attract / Certain chemicals / in).

→ ____________________

3. (by / a mosquito / have / before / You / bitten / been).

→ ____________________

4. (eggs / Female mosquitoes / need / blood / drink / to / produce / to).

→ ____________________

5. (mosquitoes / mosquito spray / from / keep / far / will / you / Using / away).

→ ____________________

Unit 02

Self-Care Technology

Vocabulary Practice

A. Write the best word for each sentence. Change its form if necessary.

serious record decide notice surgery

1. Did you ______________ that Sam was telling a lie?
2. I didn't ______________ yet which food to order.
3. I began to ______________ things to do on the calendar.
4. You must not eat anything for 12 hours before this ______________.
5. Do you agree that global warming is a ______________ problem?

B. Choose the best word for each blank.

1. How do you know whether God ______________ or not?
   a. exists b. checks c. protects d. controls
2. We have done our best to improve the quality of our ______________.
   a. issues b. moment c. products d. illnesses
3. In the hospital, doctors are prepared for a(n) ______________ at any time.
   a. fiction b. meeting c. emergency d. temperature
4. You ______________ so loudly last night that I couldn't fall asleep.
   a. woke b. snored c. drank d. drove
5. You should not believe that all the ______________ on the Internet is true.
   a. people b. monitor c. well-being d. information

C. Write the word with a similar meaning to each underlined word. Change its form if necessary.

stop meeting happen

1. Do you remember the date when the accident <u>occurred</u>? ______________
2. Greenhouses <u>prevent</u> the heated air from escaping. ______________
3. I have an important <u>appointment</u> with Mr. Peters. ______________

Writing Practice

A. Change the sentences as in the example.

Ex This is especially useful for people. They have just had surgery.
→ This is especially useful for people **who** have just had surgery.

1. The old man is in the store. He sent me flowers.
→ ______

2. Did you see the woman in the park? She looked like my boss.
→ ______

3. I went shopping with my friend. She transferred to my school last month.
→ ______

B. Match the sentence parts.

1. These products help prevent •	• a. of their health.
2. These products can send •	• b. illness by teaching people.
3. If there's an emergency, •	• c. doctors will be alerted right away.
4. She had moved a lot •	• d. the information to your doctor.
5. People might become more aware •	• e. while she was sleeping.

C. Make the sentences with the given words and write them.

1. (too / might / be / It / I / drink / much / because / coffee).
→ ______

2. (like / It / sounds / something / from / a science fiction / book).
→ ______

3. (get / start / notice / People / sick / don't / when / they / to).
→ ______

4. (She / caffeine / not / decided / to have / bedtime / before).
→ ______

5. (make / see / to / can / in / The doctor / person / an appointment / you).
→ ______

Unit 03

Earthworms

Vocabulary Practice

A. Write the best word for each sentence. Change its form if necessary.

dig   trash   loose   nature   prepare

1. You should empty the ______________ can every day.
2. The workers needed machines to ______________ a tunnel.
3. When will you start to ______________ for the mid-term exam?
4. I like this sweater's design, but it is too ______________ for me.
5. Some people believe that ______________ can heal any illness.

B. Choose the best word for each blank.

1. I didn't ______________ an umbrella, so I got wet.
   a. break   b. allow   c. bring   d. protect
2. Old tires can be ______________ in many ways.
   a. done   b. spoken   c. planted   d. recycled
3. Most plants grow well in fertile ______________.
   a. soil   b. depth   c. nutrients   d. chemicals
4. I'm trying to help the ______________ by reducing pollution.
   a. trash   b. disease   c. fertilizer   d. environment
5. Plants absorb water from the ground through their ______________.
   a. roots   b. routes   c. worms   d. burrows

C. Write the word with a similar meaning to each underlined word. Change its form if necessary.

waste   run   save

1. This stream flows into the river. ______________
2. Never throw trash on the streets or sidewalks. ______________
3. We must protect our children from harmful things. ______________

Writing Practice

A. Change the sentences as in the example.

> Ex Earthworms work very hard. They can help plants grow better.
> → Earthworms work **so** hard **that** they can help plants grow better.

1. I was very hungry. I could eat eight pieces of pizza.
   → ______________________________
2. I was too tired. I couldn't go shopping with my friends.
   → ______________________________
3. My computer was too slow. I couldn't finish my homework on time.
   → ______________________________

B. Match the sentence parts.

1. Earthworms eat the soil	•	•	a. air far down into the soil.
2. These burrows bring	•	•	b. breaking up hard soil.
3. Earthworms are good at	•	•	c. to move organic nutrients down.
4. The burrows allow rainwater	•	•	d. while they move through the earth.
5. The roots carry nutrients	•	•	e. to the plants' stems.

C. Make the sentences with the given words and write them.

1. (are / farmers / Earthworms / more / truly / than).
   → ______________________________
2. (can / This soil / be / absorbed / by / used / plants / and).
   → ______________________________
3. (into / goes / When / rains, / the water / the ground / it).
   → ______________________________
4. (the rain / prepare / Earthworms / the soil / for).
   → ______________________________
5. (trash / protect / by / the environment / recycling / Earthworms).
   → ______________________________

Unit 04

Sleep Debt

Vocabulary Practice

A. Write the best word for each sentence. Change its form if necessary.

debt   owe   task   miss   happen

1. Justin ______________ me some money.
2. Hurry up, or you will ______________ the bus.
3. The ______________ is too difficult for me to finish.
4. Ashley must pay back her ______________ to me within a month.
5. No matter what ______________, I won't change my mind.

B. Choose the best word for each blank.

1. I feel much better after a(n) ______________ sleep.
   a. tired   b. restful   c. serious   d. excited
2. Bathing after heavy exercise relieves ______________.
   a. soil   b. root   c. fatigue   d. excitement
3. That one may be cheap, but its ______________ isn't good.
   a. length   b. layout   c. height   d. quality
4. The new policy will ______________ many industries negatively.
   a. add   b. allow   c. affect   d. attack
5. The noise from the factory made me ______________.
   a. real   b. calm   c. soft   d. irritable

C. Write the word with a similar meaning to each underlined word. Change its form if necessary.

ordinary   focus   shortage

1. I cannot <u>concentrate</u> when I am nervous. ______________
2. I just want to live a happy, <u>normal</u> life. ______________
3. People in the town are worried about the <u>lack</u> of drinking water. ______________

Writing Practice

A. Change the sentences as in the example.

Ex They also make mistakes. They are doing normal tasks.
→ They also make mistakes **while doing** normal tasks.

1. I became tired. I was waiting in a long line.
→ ______________________________

2. I stayed at youth hostels. I was traveling around Europe.
→ ______________________________

3. John didn't listen to me carefully. He was packing his bag.
→ ______________________________

B. Match the sentence parts.

1. A study was done	•	• a. to high blood pressure.
2. When rats weren't allowed to sleep,	•	• b. are usually irritable.
3. People who lose just one night's sleep	•	• c. so that we can think faster.
4. Sleep helps the brain work better,	•	• d. on rats more than ten years ago.
5. Scientists say sleep debt can lead	•	• e. they died within three weeks.

C. Make the sentences with the given words and write them.

1. (A lack of sleep / affect / the quality / can / our life / of).
→ ______________________________

2. (won't / know / is / what / anymore / real / People).
→ ______________________________

3. (us / makes / restful and calm / Sleep).
→ ______________________________

4. (two nights, / concentrate / sleep / miss / If / they / for / they / can't).
→ ______________________________

5. (sleep / If / don't / enough, / you / yourself / owe / you / some rest)!
→ ______________________________

Unit 05

The Harlem Renaissance

Vocabulary Practice

A. Write the best word for each sentence. Change its form if necessary.

wit   society   inspire   movement   politics

1. Readers love the author's sense of humor and ______________.
2. These days many people are joining the well-being ______________.
3. My parents always ______________ me with their courage.
4. I major in ______________ and want to be a great politician.
5. The computer changed human ______________ in many ways.

B. Choose the best word for each blank.

1. This picture seems to ______________ your feelings.
   a. reflect   b. bring   c. appear   d. believe
2. Those books have ______________ my life in many ways.
   a. ended   b. pressed   c. depended   d. influenced
3. The novel is one of the most popular types of ______________.
   a. mood   b. poetry   c. politics   d. literature
4. The Wright brothers started to ______________ with their kite in 1899.
   a. build   b. record   c. experience   d. experiment
5. Jacob has great ______________ in his work and always does his best.
   a. class   b. pride   c. center   d. major

C. Write the word with an opposite meaning to each underlined word. Change its form if necessary.

ashamed   unknown   controlled

1. I'm <u>proud</u> of all of your achievements. ______________
2. I'm <u>independent</u> from my parents and live alone. ______________
3. The scientist became <u>well known</u> for his invention. ______________

Writing Practice

A. Change the sentences as in the example.

Ex He was influenced by jazz and blues music that were made by black people.
➜ He was influenced by jazz and blues music **made by** black people.

1. I ate a muffin that was made by Stella.
   ➜ ____________________

2. Tyler gave me some tomatoes that were grown by him.
   ➜ ____________________

3. I'm wearing a skirt that was given to me by my mother.
   ➜ ____________________

B. Match the sentence parts.

1. Zora believed black Americans	•	• a. of poor and homeless black people.
2. It was a period	•	• b. to tell the world about her culture.
3. He spoke out in support	•	• c. could be free and independent.
4. He became an important part	•	• d. when African-Americans did great things.
5. As she grew up, she wanted	•	• e. of the Harlem Renaissance.

C. Make the sentences with the given words and write them.

1. (her race / was / She / of / proud).
   ➜ ____________________

2. (the center / Harlem / black middle class / of / became / a growing).
   ➜ ____________________

3. (He / 13 / at / of / started / writing / the age / poetry).
   ➜ ____________________

4. (tried / the mood / the times / of / in / his work / to / reflect / He).
   ➜ ____________________

5. (helped / experiment / This music / him / rhythm and free verse / with).
   ➜ ____________________

Unit 06 **Ballet**

Vocabulary Practice

A. Write the best word for each sentence. Change its form if necessary.

feature   public   company   royalty   fancy

1. Gold is traditionally a symbol of ______________.
2. You must have better manners in ______________ places.
3. This summer's fashions ______________ brilliant colors.
4. Jackie was wearing a ______________ stage costume.
5. David has been working for this ______________ for 20 years.

B. Choose the best word for each blank.

1. The folks in ______________ clothes all danced together.
   a. equal   b. racial   c. middle   d. traditional
2. It is said that human beings ______________ from apes.
   a. drew   b. decided   c. evolved   d. accepted
3. We're planning to ______________ a factory in China.
   a. compete   b. feature   c. perform   d. establish
4. The child screamed when he saw the man in the Halloween ______________.
   a. tale   b. costume   c. gesture   d. nation
5. The delicious food and a(n) ______________ view make this place like heaven.
   a. effective   b. essential   c. frightening   d. impressive

C. Write the word with a similar meaning to each underlined word. Change its form if necessary.

show   special   start

1. The dance academy held a special Christmas <u>performance</u>. ______________
2. This animal is <u>unique</u> to South America. ______________
3. We are planning to <u>establish</u> a factory in China. ______________

Writing Practice

A. Change the sentences as in the example.

Ex King Louis XIV of France founded the first school of dance.
➔ The first school of dance **was founded by** King Louis XIV of France.

1. My aunt opened the Italian restaurant.
➔ ______________________________

2. My father invented the special dish.
➔ ______________________________

3. The woman made these beaded necklaces.
➔ ______________________________

B. Match the sentence parts.

1. Ballet could be enjoyed • • a. was opened in Paris.
2. It featured ballet as part • • b. by the public.
3. They would hold dance performances • • c. based on traditional folk dances.
4. The first opera house • • d. of the opera performances.
5. They were competing to see • • e. who could have impressive shows.

C. Make the sentences with the given words and write them.

1. (is / one / dance / of / the most / forms / popular / Ballet / of).
➔ ______________________________

2. (from / held / European royalty / dances / for / evolved / It).
➔ ______________________________

3. (costumes and backgrounds / fancy / featured / These / shows).
➔ ______________________________

4. (are / around / There / the world / ballet companies / cities / in).
➔ ______________________________

5. (dancers / the special skills / for / in / instructed / ballet / needed / It).
➔ ______________________________

Unit 07

Life in Space

Vocabulary Practice

A. Write the best word for each sentence. Change its form if necessary.

station effect heat float space

1. Oil will ______________ on water.
2. Someday it might not expensive to travel to ______________.
3. ______________ the rice in the microwave before you eat it.
4. This medicine didn't have any ______________ on me.
5. I arrived at the ______________ the moment the train left.

B. Choose the best word for each blank.

1. ______________ the vegetables under running water.
   a. Wear b. Wipe c. Dress d. Rinse
2. Ellen likes to ______________ that she is a princess.
   a. contain b. reflect c. imagine d. become
3. You can ______________ more sugar if you want it to taste sweeter.
   a. add b. reduce c. wash d. purchase
4. In NASA, ______________ need to undergo hundreds of hours of training.
   a. goods b. authors c. shuttles d. astronauts
5. Kate often can't ______________ her anger and shouts at people.
   a. fly b. contain c. travel d. control

C. Write the word with an opposite meaning to each underlined word. Change its form if necessary.

sink loosen usual

1. Amy wears <u>special</u> clothes when she goes on a picnic. ______________
2. The little girl is learning to <u>tie</u> the laces of her shoes. ______________
3. The sailor found a little boat <u>floating</u> on the river. ______________

Writing Practice

A. Change the sentences as in the example.

Ex They wash themselves with special soap. It doesn't have to be rinsed off.
→ They wash themselves with special soap **that** doesn't have to be rinsed off.

1. I'll give you a handout. It can be useful for understanding this class.
→ ______________________________

2. Michael made a special dish. It could be served at a restaurant.
→ ______________________________

3. You have to read the textbook. It can be borrowed from the library.
→ ______________________________

B. Match the sentence parts.

1. The ISS is like •	• a. the effects of gravity.
2. Their life in space is different •	• b. clean with towels.
3. The astronauts don't feel •	• c. a big house in space.
4. Astronauts dress the same way •	• d. as people on the Earth.
5. They wipe their bodies •	• e. from life on the Earth.

C. Make the sentences with the given words and write them.

1. (the same food / eat / Astronauts / that / eat / in / space / the Earth / people / on).
→ ______________________________

2. (they / the food / in / an oven / heat / Sometimes).
→ ______________________________

3. (in / wash / space / need / themselves / to / Astronauts).
→ ______________________________

4. (computers / The atmosphere / is / by / controlled / in / the space station).
→ ______________________________

5. (themselves / have / Astronauts / to / tie / down / to / going / before / bed).
→ ______________________________

Unit 08

Green City

Vocabulary Practice

A. Write the best word for each sentence. Change its form if necessary.

comfortable   develop   natural   plan   protection

1. These wide shoes are ______________ to me.
2. ______________ my trip to America makes me happy.
3. I can make soap using ______________ materials.
4. The company's workers are trying to ______________ new products.
5. It is said that spicy food provides ______________ against food poisoning.

B. Choose the best word for each blank.

1. Emily decided to ______________ her grades at school.
   a. deal   b. relate   c. improve   d. response
2. Cities filled with smog are threatening the ______________ system.
   a. free   b. planning   c. business   d. ecological
3. Cars and factories are mainly responsible for air ______________.
   a. cleaner   b. energy   c. pollution   d. connection
4. Global warming is a big threat to the ______________.
   a. map   b. solution   c. recyling   d. environment
5. The major ______________ of a blog is to share one's thoughts.
   a. lesson   b. problem   c. function   d. well-being

C. Write the word with a similar meaning to each underlined word. Change its form if necessary.

develop   answers   surroundings

1. I'm trying to find better <u>solutions</u>. ______________
2. Ethan studied really hard to <u>improve</u> his English skills. ______________
3. People are strongly affected by their <u>environment</u>. ______________

Writing Practice

A. Change the sentences as in the example.

Ex There is a relationship between green areas and the places. People live there.
→ There is a relationship between green areas and the places **where** people live.

1. I visited the town. I was born there.
→ ______________________________

2. I like to stay in quiet places. Almost nobody else lives there.
→ ______________________________

3. I returned to the point. I started from there.
→ ______________________________

B. Match the sentence parts.

1. Animals can easily move •	• a. to build buildings.
2. Stockholm has used land •	• b. used to improve the soil.
3. The city leaders planned •	• c. from one area to another.
4. Food waste from homes can be •	• d. more comfortable.
5. The green areas make people's lives •	• e. the ecological protection areas carefully.

C. Make the sentences with the given words and write them.

1. (of / a great deal / has / beauty / natural / Stockholm).
→ ______________________________

2. (important / is / of / lessons / that / is / planning / the biggest / One).
→ ______________________________

3. (go / this / kind of / Using / planning, / can / more cities / green).
→ ______________________________

4. (these protected areas / close / They / tried / each other / to / put / to).
→ ______________________________

5. (Most / pollution / the land / of / is / from / free).
→ ______________________________

Unit 09

Xylitol

Vocabulary Practice

A. Write the best word for each sentence. Change its form if necessary.

decay chew prove material infection

1. Dancers wear clothes made of flexible ______________.
2. It was ______________ that Jackson was the thief.
3. Plastic bags take a long time to ______________.
4. In some countries, people can't ______________ gum in public places.
5. Washing your hands is the best way to prevent ______________.

B. Choose the best word for each blank.

1. This chocolate cupcake tastes very ______________.
   a. sour b. sweet c. harmful d. popular
2. I can show you a sample of our new ______________.
   a. product b. disease c. nature d. diabetes
3. It is the duty of the police to ______________ crimes.
   a. taste b. infect c. prevent d. discover
4. I'm sure that this project will bring many ______________ to us.
   a. chemists b. benefits c. grounds d. criminals
5. My professor told me that I need more ______________ on this topic.
   a. clue b. speech c. addition d. research

C. Write the word with an opposite meaning to each underlined word. Change its form if necessary.

minor unusual increase

1. I try to keep a <u>regular</u> schedule every day. ______________
2. The medicine will <u>decrease</u> the number of bacteria. ______________
3. Sleepiness was a <u>major</u> factor in the accident. ______________

Writing Practice

A. Change the sentences as in the example.

Ex Gum made with xylitol is as safe as gum made with sugar.
→ Gum made with xylitol is **safer than** gum made with sugar.

1. This radio is as expensive as that table.
→ ______________________________

2. Cats are as friendly as dogs.
→ ______________________________

3. Learning to ride a bike is as easy as walking.
→ ______________________________

B. Match the sentence parts.

1. Xylitol is popular •	• a. blood sugar levels.
2. Xylitol was first discovered •	• b. from regular gum.
3. Xylitol was shown •	• c. among people with diabetes.
4. Xylitol doesn't affect •	• d. to prevent tooth decay.
5. It didn't taste any different •	• e. by German and French chemists.

C. Make the sentences with the given words and write them.

1. (them / Other products / keep / with / xylitol / in / us / healthy).
→ ______________________________

2. (why / gum companies / xylitol / use / many / is / This).
→ ______________________________

3. (sugar lovers / liked / its discovery, / xylitol / its taste / have / Since / for).
→ ______________________________

4. (in / xylitol / fight / off / The materials / harmful / bacteria).
→ ______________________________

5. (Xylitol / been / has / to / be / proven / safe and healthy).
→ ______________________________

Musical Instruments

Vocabulary Practice

A. Write the best word for each sentence. Change its form if necessary.

wonder	blow	confuse	instrument	variety

1. The trumpet is a kind of wind ______________.
2. I ______________ if you received my message.
3. I was ______________ when the man shouted at me suddenly.
4. The wind ______________ so hard that it broke the window.
5. I left my hometown for a(n) ______________ of reasons.

B. Choose the best word for each blank.

1. The earthquake caused the building to ______________.
   a. prove b. draw c. vibrate d. repeat
2. I put the books in the box and tied it with ______________.
   a. bow b. hole c. reed d. string
3. The man ______________ the table with a white cloth.
   a. played b. rubbed c. attended d. expressed
4. In nature, animals and plants find ways to live in ______________.
   a. sum b. sound c. danger d. harmony
5. I don't think ______________ e-books are more convenient than paper books.
   a. modern b. classic c. mental d. musical

C. Write the word with a similar meaning to each underlined word. Change its form if necessary.

make	shake	visit

1. My house <u>vibrated</u> when there was a thunder storm. ______________
2. Our team will <u>produce</u> many new ideas for the company. ______________
3. Nobody <u>attended</u> the seminar, so the room was empty. ______________

Writing Practice

A. Change the sentences as in the example.

Ex The percussion instruments produce a sound when they are hit or shaken.
→ The percussion instruments produce a sound **when hit or shaken**.

1. She often talks while she is sleeping.
→ ______

2. I usually burst into tears when I am extremely scared.
→ ______

3. Tyler listens to his mom carefully when he is scolded.
→ ______

B. Match the sentence parts.

1. There are three groups •	• a. with their fingers to make sounds.
2. People may confuse •	• b. of instruments in a modern orchestra.
3. The sound of brass comes •	• c. from the players' lips vibrating.
4. The sound is created •	• d. when the player blows into the reed.
5. The players cover holes •	• e. the brass and woodwinds.

C. Make the sentences with the given words and write them.

1. (of / played / being / What / kinds / instruments / were / musical)?
→ ______

2. (are / and / String instruments / of / wood / made / four strings / have).
→ ______

3. (played / four-string instruments / the same / All / are / way).
→ ______

4. (instruments / an orchestra / the percussion / The third group / of / in / is).
→ ______

5. (a close look / Don't / to / the instruments / at / take / forget).
→ ______

Unit 11

Yellow Dust

Vocabulary Practice

A. Write the best word for each sentence. Change its form if necessary.

carry poisonous ash economy ruin

1. Some flowers are beautiful but ______________.
2. ______________ from the fire blew in to my garden.
3. If you sit too close to the TV, you're going to ______________ your eyes.
4. Many people lost their jobs because of the poor ______________.
5. Rats ______________ many types of diseases and spread them to humans.

B. Choose the best word for each blank.

1. How much did it ______________ to produce the movie?
   a. cost b. attract c. affect d. breathe
2. Too much rain can be ______________ for some crops.
   a. dusty b. enough c. creative d. harmful
3. I have a ______________ throat because of a cold.
   a. cold b. sour c. sore d. sound
4. The old building was ______________ by the fire.
   a. caused b. cleaned c. avoided d. destroyed
5. The ground is too hard to ______________ trees now.
   a. plant b. draw c. affect d. control

C. Write the word with a similar meaning to each underlined word. Change its form if necessary.

bad disease happen

1. Many mysterious things <u>occur</u> in that town. ______________
2. Not all TV programs are <u>harmful</u> to teenagers. ______________
3. If you wait too long, it will be difficult to treat your <u>illness</u>. ______________

Writing Practice

A. Change the sentences as in the example.

Ex Yellow dust is unwelcome because it has many harmful effects.

➜ Yellow dust is unwelcome **because of** its many harmful effects.

1. My flight was delayed because it snowed heavily.

   ➜ ______________________________

2. I couldn't come here on time because the traffic was too heavy.

   ➜ ______________________________

3. I cannot hear what you are saying because I have a problem with my ears.

   ➜ ______________________________

B. Match the sentence parts.

1. The wind carries the dust •
2. Others stay home to avoid •
3. People even die of illnesses •
4. Yellow dust storms cost •
5. Some people wear •

• a. people a lot of money.
• b. masks when they go outside.
• c. over China, Korea, and Japan.
• d. breathing the bad air.
• e. that are caused by yellow dust.

C. Make the sentences with the given words and write them.

1. (full / as / is / of / Yellow dust / pollution / such / ash).

   ➜ ______________________________

2. (the environment / harm / the soil / ruining / The dust / by / can) .

   ➜ ______________________________

3. (How / yellow dust / with / deal / we / can)?

   ➜ ______________________________

4. (need / down / pollution / on / cut / We / to).

   ➜ ______________________________

5. (can / to / 6,000 gallons / water / to / up / take / of / It / clean / one jumbo jet).

   ➜ ______________________________

Unit 12

Fruits and Vegetables

Vocabulary Practice

A. Write the best word for each sentence. Change its form if necessary.

risk   cancer   nutrient   memory   avoid

1. We left early to ______________ rush hour traffic.
2. Many people are afraid to take ______________.
3. Heavy smokers are more likely to have lung ______________.
4. People's ______________ don't always work perfectly.
5. The roots of plants absorb water and ______________ from the soil.

B. Choose the best word for each blank.

1. Does the price ______________ a service charge?

   a. add   b. reject   c. include   d. multiply

2. Do you want fruit-flavored or just ______________ yogurt?

   a. thin   b. plain   c. various   d. harmful

3. Garlic is believed to control high blood ______________.

   a. cell   b. pressure   c. stomach   d. sickness

4. My aunt is ______________ with her third child now.

   a. pregnant   b. healthy   c. irritable   d. dependent

5. Eating too much fat can cause serious ______________ problems.

   a. cure   b. disease   c. memory   d. cholesterol

C. Write the word with a similar meaning to each underlined word. Change its form if necessary.

include   improve   skill

1. Hot springs often <u>contain</u> many minerals. ______________
2. I think this task is beyond my <u>ability</u>. ______________
3. I was told to enjoy outdoor activities to <u>strengthen</u> my heart. ______________

Writing Practice

A. Change the sentences as in the example.

Ex Green fruits include plant chemicals. They help you avoid eye disease.
➡ Green fruits include plant chemicals **that** help you avoid eye disease.

1. My friend and I ate lunch at a restaurant. It is famous for its sandwiches.
➡ ______________________________

2. I was born in a town. It is famous for its friendliness.
➡ ______________________________

3. On my way home I saw a poster for a musical. It will start next month.
➡ ______________________________

B. Match the sentence parts.

1. Orange fruits strengthen ability • • a. against cancer.
2. White fruits and vegetables • • b. to help prevent sickness.
3. Orange and yellow fruits fight • • c. different nutrients.
4. Food scientists say you must • • d. eat different colored fruits.
5. The different colors contain • • e. improve cholesterol levels.

C. Make the sentences with the given words and write them.

1. (reduces / Red fruits / the risk / lycopene, / of / which / cancer / contain).
➡ ______________________________

2. (Orange / your eyes / healthy / make / help / fruits and vegetables).
➡ ______________________________

3. (good / are / pregnant / Green / for / mothers / fruits and vegetables).
➡ ______________________________

4. (fruits and vegetables / the body cells / protect / Blue and purple).
➡ ______________________________

5. (against / White / stomach cancer / fruits and vegetables / fight).
➡ ______________________________

Unit 13

Ancient Money

Vocabulary Practice

A. Write the best word for each sentence. Change its form if necessary.

express metal own wealth expensive

1. You need a license to ______________ a gun in the U.K.
2. Some people ______________ their feelings through music.
3. It is not ______________ that makes me happy.
4. This helmet is made of ______________ and is very hard.
5. I can't buy these shoes because they are too ______________.

B. Choose the best word for each blank.

1. I think it is a good idea to save some money for the ______________.
   a. value b. credit c. public d. future
2. The first electric light was ______________ by Humphry Davy in 1800.
   a. carried b. thrown c. invented d. purchased
3. The company keeps a high ______________ of quality.
   a. outfit b. source c. material d. standard
4. I ______________ my old chair for this sweater at the flea market.
   a. treated b. traded c. bought d. realized
5. A strange ______________ caught my eye in the dark.
   a. object b. credit c. subject d. symbol

C. Write the word with a similar meaning to each underlined word. Change its form if necessary.

show usual worth

1. Jim sent his uncle a letter to <u>express</u> his gratitude. ______________
2. You seem to know the true <u>value</u> of hard work. ______________
3. These days, email is much more <u>common</u> than letters. ______________

Writing Practice

A. Change the sentences as in the example.

Ex There's no telling. What will money be like in the future?

➡ There's no telling **what money will be** like in the future.

1. I don't know. Who sent me this email?

➡ ______________________________

2. Kate never answered. Why didn't she come to the seminar?

➡ ______________________________

3. Nobody knew. Who won the first prize?

➡ ______________________________

B. Match the sentence parts.

1. People have always tried • • a. from paper money.
2. Over time, we have changed • • b. to trade for jewerly or rice.
3. Paper is more common • • c. than expensive metals like gold.
4. You had to bring your cows • • d. how we express the value of things.
5. We seem to be moving away • • e. to set standards about the value of objects.

C. Make the sentences with the given words and write them.

1. (do / How / the value / of / you / something / know)?

➡ ______________________________

2. (The number / wealth / your / was / of / cows / a symbol / of / owned / you).

➡ ______________________________

3. (shells / The Chinese / of / a kind / used / as / money).

➡ ______________________________

4. (is / China / where / invented / paper money / was).

➡ ______________________________

5. (what / It / to carry / easier / coins / to / was / show / owned / they).

➡ ______________________________

Unit 14 Social Network Service

Vocabulary Practice

A. Write the best word for each sentence. Change its form if necessary.

privacy connect social effort share

1. Henry is very ______________ and loves meeting new people.
2. It is very difficult for stars to protect their ______________.
3. The workers made a great ______________ to finish the building on time.
4. Dan decided to ______________ the housework with his wife.
5. Can you show me how to ______________ to the Internet?

B. Choose the best word for each blank.

1. This show is being ______________ live.
   a. asked b. called c. showed d. broadcast
2. Do you have laundry ______________ in this hotel?
   a. level b. service c. device d. program
3. I ______________ a new notice on the board.
   a. met b. meant c. built d. posted
4. A cold can ______________ into all kinds of illnesses.
   a. move b. invent c. develop d. imagine
5. The local ______________ formed a close bond between them.
   a. issue b. technology c. community d. information

C. Write the word with a similar meaning to each underlined word. Change its form if necessary.

talk help private

1. You cannot ask any <u>personal</u> questions. ______________
2. I used to <u>chat</u> with Jim for a while after school. ______________
3. Emily is planning to <u>support</u> her elderly aunt who lives alone. ______________

Writing Practice

A. Change the sentences as in the example.

Ex People think that there are over 200 active SNSs.
→ **It is thought that** there are over 200 active SNSs.

1. People say that eating breakfast is important.
→ ____________________

2. People expect that our team will win the game.
→ ____________________

3. People think that we have to respect elders.
→ ____________________

B. Match the sentence parts.

1. Users must be careful •   • a. they can share it with anyone.
2. SNSs make it easy for us •   • b. about what information they post.
3. Users would communicate •   • c. to connect with anyone.
4. Two of the most popular ones •   • d. by sharing photos online.
5. As soon as they think of something, •   • e. are Facebook and Twitter.

C. Make the sentences with the given words and write them.

1. (better / have / features / and / to / use / easier / are / They).
→ ____________________

2. (helps / build / It / people / personal / stronger / relationships).
→ ____________________

3. (you're / with / like / a close / may / It / seem / chatting / friend).
→ ____________________

4. (thousands of / viewed / be / message / Your / can / people / by).
→ ____________________

5. (allow / These services / to / their thoughts / people / broadcast).
→ ____________________

Unit 15

Art Therapy

Vocabulary Practice

A. Write the best word for each sentence. Change its form if necessary.

deal   figure   physically   heal   express

1. I can't ______________ out why this computer won't work.
2. Yoga can ______________ both the body and the mind.
3. We need to ______________ with the most urgent problem first.
4. I'd like to ______________ my gratitude to everyone who helped me.
5. Noah is ______________ challenged, but he never gave up on his dreams.

B. Choose the best word for each blank.

1. The ______________ is as important as the result.
   a. process   b. treatment   c. expression   d. introduction
2. You'd better take medicine to ______________ your pain.
   a. ease   b. bring   c. develop   d. disappear
3. Ryan gave a(n) ______________ answer to my question.
   a. less   b. mental   c. harmful   d. unrelated
4. It is said that there is no ______________ for diabetes.
   a. care   b. cure   c. problem   d. reduction
5. I was happy to ______________ his greeting card and warm message.
   a. float   b. receive   c. enjoy   d. release

C. Write the word with a similar meaning to each underlined word. Change its form if necessary.

surprisingly   treat   slowly

1. My puppy can jump <u>amazingly</u> high. ______________
2. The train <u>gradually</u> disappeared into the darkness. ______________
3. It's too late to be able to <u>cure</u> my disease easily. ______________

Writing Practice

A. Change the sentences as in the example.

Ex To find anything unrelated to art is hard in our lives.

➡ **It** is hard **to find** anything unrelated to art in our lives.

1. To get up early in the morning isn't easy.

   ➡ ______________________________

2. To express my thoughts isn't difficult.

   ➡ ______________________________

3. To meet new people is interesting.

   ➡ ______________________________

B. Match the sentence parts.

1. It is a fun activity •	• a. on society.
2. Art has had a strong influence •	• b. how patients feel.
3. The paintings show •	• c. expressing themselves with words.
4. Patients have a hard time •	• d. that can help pass the time.
5. Repeating this process •	• e. gradually eases patients' problems.

C. Make the sentences with the given words and write them.

1. (sick / mentally / Art / to / can / be / treat / used / people).

   ➡ ______________________________

2. (problems / The therapists / out / patients' / try / figure / to).

   ➡ ______________________________

3. (being / Art therapy / to / is / patients / as / cure / a way / developed).

   ➡ ______________________________

4. (therapy / is / It / thought to / one of / forms of / be / the best).

   ➡ ______________________________

5. (with / patients / creative tools / stress / with / helps / deal / Painting).

   ➡ ______________________________

Unit 16

Threatened Oceans

Vocabulary Practice

A. Write the best word for each sentence. Change its form if necessary.

drought dump introduce spill damage

1. You must not ______________ trash in this area.
2. Could you clean up the ______________ on the floor?
3. I checked out the ______________ to my car from the accident.
4. The stream seems have be dried up because of the ______________.
5. The school needs to ______________ a new system for effective time management.

B. Choose the best word for each blank.

1. The advertisement had a(n) ______________ on sales.
   a. affect b. effect c. number d. variety
2. Patrick said that his business is in a tough ______________.
   a. species b. source c. amount d. situation
3. China is the ______________ habitat of giant pandas.
   a. native b. negative c. creative d. dangerous
4. You have to understand the exact reality you're ______________.
   a. fixing b. facing c. creating d. releasing
5. If there was no water, no one could ______________.
   a. save b. cause c. appear d. survive

C. Write the word with a similar meaning to each underlined word. Change its form if necessary.

rise severe weather

1. The <u>climate</u> in Ireland is generally mild. ______________
2. I have <u>extreme</u> stress at work. ______________
3. I heard that the price of basic goods would <u>increase</u> again. ______________

Writing Practice

A. Change the sentences as in the example.

Ex We have to take just one step to be able to save our oceans.
→ **If** we take just one step, we **might be** able to save our oceans.

1. I have to make an effort to get a good result.
→ ______________________________

2. Joey has to be more patient to be a nice person.
→ ______________________________

3. I have to get some rest to get well soon.
→ ______________________________

B. Match the sentence parts.

1. It introduced non-native species •	• a. from happening.
2. Native species find it •	• b. that are hard to solve.
3. We can prevent further damage •	• c. the balance of the ecosystem.
4. These jellyfish have destroyed •	• d. to the Mediterranean Sea.
5. These materials create problems •	• e. difficult to survive.

C. Make the sentences with the given words and write them.

1. (into / Factories / materials / the sea / harmful / release).
→ ______________________________

2. (sea animals / Many / died / have / of / these spills / because).
→ ______________________________

3. (have / There / a large number / oil spills / been / of / oceans / in).
→ ______________________________

4. (need / People / understand / to / the dangerous situation / face / oceans / our).
→ ______________________________

5. (Atlantic bluefin tuna / It's / too many / have / because / fisherman / caught).
→ ______________________________

Word List

Unit 01

- bite
- spread
- disease
- female
- produce
- attract
- sensor
- visual
- detect
- avoid

Unit 02

- snore
- rate
- decide
- exist
- record
- information
- appointment
- alert
- notice
- aware

Unit 03

- soil
- fertile
- absorb
- prepare
- flow
- loose
- protect
- recycle
- trash
- nature

Unit 04

- owe
- allow
- lack
- affect
- irritable
- fatigue
- concentrate
- normal
- debt
- recover

Unit 05

- movement
- literature
- proud
- race
- independent
- wit
- experiment
- reflect
- mood
- influence

Unit 06

- evolve
- royalty
- compete

- impressive
- luxurious
- found
- instruct
- public
- establish
- nation

Unit 07

- astronaut
- effect
- gravity
- float
- container
- add
- atmosphere
- control
- wipe
- tie

Unit 08

- natural
- pollution
- balance
- environment
- develop
- area
- function
- relationship
- improve
- solution

Unit 09

- chew
- regular
- discover
- benefit
- research
- prevent
- decay
- infection
- material
- prove

Unit 10

- wonder
- instrument
- modern
- harmony
- string
- confuse
- blow
- vibrate
- variety
- attend

Unit 11

- carry
- harmful
- ash
- poisonous
- occur
- illness
- destroy

- habitat
- cost
- major

Unit 12

- plain
- contain
- nutrient
- role
- reduce
- risk
- strengthen
- ability
- include
- pregnant

Unit 13

- value
- standard
- object
- express
- own
- symbol
- trade
- realize
- invent
- common

Unit 14

- social
- support
- effort
- chat
- share
- broadcast
- personal
- post
- view
- border

Unit 15

- mentally
- physically
- cure
- heal
- deal
- figure
- repeat
- gradually
- ease
- receive

Unit 16

- increase
- threaten
- spill
- release
- extreme
- climate
- drought
- damage
- situation
- dump

Aqua

Reading Peak Aqua is a three-level nonfiction reading series designed for intermediate to high intermediate students. Compelling topics motivate students and make reading exercises informative and meaningful. This series presents background knowledge passages to ensure a better understanding of topics while engaging the interest of readers. All readings are based on carefully considered word lists to expand students' vocabulary and develop their reading fluency. This series includes reading comprehension questions to enhance students' critical thinking skills. With *Reading Peak Aqua*, students are ready to become advanced readers.

Features:

- Engaging, academic nonfiction readings in various forms of writing
- Interesting, informative background knowledge
- Exercises to improve reading speed
- Open-ended questions that strengthen students' thinking and writing skills
- Basic reading strategies accompanied by simple exercises
- Level-appropriate word lists and definitions before each main reading
- Graphic organizers to support students' mind mapping abilities
- Workbook for more vocabulary, grammar, and writing practice

Components:

Student Book / Workbook / Audio CD

Online Resources: www.nebooks.co.kr (Korean) / www.nebuildandgrow.com (English)

MP3 files / Vocabulary lists / Answer keys and translations

Reading Peak Aqua Series:

[190~210 words]

[220~240 words]

[250~270 words]

Category	Title	Lexile	Components
	Insight Link 1,2,3	500L-610L	Student Book/ Workbook/ MultiROM
	Insight Link 4,5,6	670L-760L	Student Book/ Workbook/ MultiROM
	Subject Link Starter 1,2,3	430L-460L	Student Book/ Workbook/ MultiROM
	Subject Link 1,2,3	520L-610L	Student Book/ Workbook/ Audio CD
	Subject Link 4,5,6	720L-830L	Student Book/ Workbook/ Audio CD
	Subject Link 7,8,9	860L-950L	Student Book/ Workbook/ Audio CD
Listening	Listening Stage Starter 1,2,3		Student Book/ Workbook/ Scripts & Answer Keys/ MultiROM
	Listening Stage 1,2,3		Student Book/ Workbook/ Scripts & Answer Keys/ MultiROM
	Listening Seed 1,2,3		Student Book/ Workbook/ Scripts & Answer Keys/ MP3 CD
	Listening Season 1,2,3 [2nd Edition]		Student Book/ Workbook/ Scripts & Answer Keys/ MultiROM
	Listening Planner 1,2,3		Student Book/ Workbook/ Scripts & Answer Keys/ MP3 CD
Writing	Write Right Beginner 1,2,3		Student Book/ Workbook
	Write Right 1,2,3		Student Book/ Workbook
	Write Right Paragraph to Essay 1,2,3		Student Book/ Workbook
Speaking	Everyone, Speak! Kids 1,2,3		Student Book/ Workbook/ MultiROM
	Everyone, Speak! Beginner 1,2,3		Student Book/ Workbook/ MultiROM
	Everyone, Speak! 1,2,3		Student Book/ Workbook/ MultiROM
Grammar	Grammar Space Kids 1,2,3		Student Book/ Workbook
	Grammar Space Beginner 1,2,3		Student Book/ Workbook
	Grammar Space 1,2,3		Student Book/ Workbook
	Grammar in Mind 1,2,3		Student Book/ Workbook
	Grammar in Focus 1,2,3		Student Book/ Workbook/ Audio CD
	Grammar Effect 1,2,3		Student Book/ Workbook/ Answer Keys